Thank

W9-CUX-246

Michael Knepp
2016

TROUTSMITH

Terrace Books, a trade imprint of the University of Wisconsin Press, takes its name from the Memorial Union Terrace, located at the University of Wisconsin–Madison. Since its inception in 1907, the Wisconsin Union has provided a venue for students, faculty, staff, and alumni to debate art, music, politics, and the issues of the day. It is a place where theater, music, drama, literature, dance, outdoor activities, and major speakers are made available to the campus and the community. To learn more about the Union, visit www.union.wisc.edu.

TROUTSMITH

An Angler's Tales and Travels

KEVIN SEAROCK

TERRACE BOOKS

A trade imprint of the University of Wisconsin Press

Terrace Books
A trade imprint of the University of Wisconsin Press
1930 Monroe Street, 3rd Floor
Madison, Wisconsin 53711-2059
uwpress.wisc.edu

3 Henrietta Street
London WC2E 8LU, England
eurospanbookstore.com

Printed in the United States of America

Library of Congress Cataloging-in-Publication Data

Searock, Kevin.
Troutsmith: an angler's tales and travels / Kevin Searock.
        p.   cm.
ISBN 978-0-299-29370-3 (cloth: alk. paper)
ISBN 978-0-299-29373-4 (e-book)
    1. Fishing.   2. Fishing—Wisconsin.   I. Title.
SH441.S455 2013
799.12—dc23
2012032686

A version of "Tiger of the Valleys," titled "Jewels of the Flow," appeared in the Spring 2005
issue of *Wisconsin Outdoor Journal*; "Spiders and Flies" appeared in the Spring 2006 issue of
Wisconsin Outdoor Journal and in the March 2006 issue of *Midwest Fly Fishing*; a version of
"Spring Ponds," titled "Kicking for Pond Trout," appeared in the May 2006 issue of *Wisconsin
Outdoor Journal*; "Auld Red" appeared in the February/March 2007 issue of *Gray's Sporting
Journal*; "The Black Trout of English Run" appeared in the September/October 2007 issue of
Wisconsin Trails; a version of "Dame's Rocket" is published online at www.flyfishingwis.com.

For Teresa,

who says she never said,

"Give a man a fish and he eats for a day;
teach a man to fish and you never see him again,"

but she knows it's true.

Contents

Preface

The first thing a student of magic learns is that there are books about magic and books of magic. And the second thing he learns is that a perfectly respectable example of the former may be had for two or three guineas at a good bookseller, and that the value of the latter is above rubies.

Susanna Clarke

I wanted to write a book of fishing, because fishing is water-magic: irrational, seductive, powerful, and dangerous. Too many lives are irrevocably changed by time spent near water. Too many ordinary-looking people we pass by on the street are really thralls; their eyes seem focused on the here and now, but their minds are haunted by the siren song of water crashing down from high country, or booming to the shore of some lonely beach. They wish to be elsewhere. I am one of them.

I've devoted my life to fishing in the same way that other, wiser people have devoted their lives to sculpture or the piano. Fishing is my art: an exercise of great skill acquired slowly over more than forty years of devoted study and practice. This makes it hard for me to work with beginners. People ask me questions like "How do you cast so that the lure lands on the *exact* spot that you're looking at?" or "How did you know that the fish had taken the fly?" and I'm embarrassed because I can't explain how I do these things. Or maybe I'm afraid that the answers aren't what twenty-first-century people want to hear. In a world where knowledge and information are just a click or two away, wisdom can be gained only through the hard lessons of experience, and experience needs time.

None of us spends as much time in the outdoors as we'd like, but the next best thing is sharing stories with other kindred spirits. So come fishing with me if you dare, but be on your guard. It is a terribly fine line between a passion for fishing and an obsession. I fish because I'm driven to by something deep within, because I can't not fish. Days on the water with me can begin at first light and end long after sunset. Such days are hungry, thirsty, wind burned, and footsore. They are also rich and unforgettable adventures. There's no telling where the quest for fish may take us and I can't guarantee your safety. We'll travel a fair way across this good earth, and find that despite its problems this is still a beautiful world filled with miracles. We'll fall in with a few good friends, the best men and women I know. We'll encounter some legendary fish, and perhaps even bring a few old battle-wagons to the net.

There's a story about a bent, wrinkled old man who could usually be seen fishing from atop a stone bridge in a little village. Only in winter would he desert his post on the bridge, and his return in spring was as sure as the trill of a red-winged blackbird or a crocus pushing through last year's leaves. In season the villagers got used to seeing his hunched form leaning over the parapet, studying the depths of the pool below, pondering the fate of worm or minnow suspended beneath his handmade quill float. Though never a talker, the angler always had a smile or a friendly wave for passers-by. Finally one day a child asked him the pivotal question "What are you fishing for?" The angler smiled, and then he answered with just a single word, "Memories."

Durwards Glen, Wisconsin, 2012

SHORT CASTS—WISCONSIN

After Work

He fairly flew out of work at the end of the day. It was one of the first warm, sunny afternoons of the year, and spring fever had hit him just as hard as it did when he was sixteen, knocking him for a loop and sending him back to something like adolescence. The state highway took him fifteen miles south, to the village where John Muir had lived once. With the truck's windows rolled down and the CD player blaring he sang at the top of his lungs, crazy, off-key accompaniments to Neil Young, wailed like a banshee. His wife would have been horrified. His students would have laughed. John Muir would have understood.

He parked near the ruins of the old mill dam. Downstream the little creek meandered through sandy bottoms and thickets of tag alder until it finally lost itself in the Wisconsin River, but upstream where it cut through a glacial moraine the stream splashed noisily over a rocky bed, bubbling and gurgling through a series of classic pools, riffles, and runs. Today was an upstream day. He'd save the swamps below for the long June twilights, when the big *Hexagenia* mayflies fluttered clumsily in the gloaming and hook-jawed old brown trout began looking up with hungry, merciless stares.

Still whistling, he unzipped the double rod case and chose his weapon; a light, limber 7½-foot fly rod that took a #4 double-tapered line. He loved that little rod; he loved the strong, fruity smell of the Chinese quince burl reel seat and the glow of its nickel-silver fittings; loved the way it balanced with a fine English fly reel, seeming almost weightless in his hands. He strung up the rod and knotted a two-fly rig to the end of the tapered leader, a heavily weighted scud fly in the lead, followed by a smaller, green-throated and grouse-hackled caddis larva. One fly for dead drifting and the other for "induced takes"—that quick, subtle lift of the rod that he'd learned from old Jimmy Leisenring on the Little Lehigh, in that long ago Pennsylvania of his youth.

Killdeer bobbing on the grass, robins fluttering in the thickets along the stream, and then the dark, mossy green water boiling past the rocks in its stony bed: a classic trout stream in miniature, like so many Wisconsin trout waters. Cautiously he waded out into the tail of the mill pool. He moved like a heron—smooth, slow, and noiseless. He raised the rod, and like magic the line began to unroll across the long pool. Small movements of his hands, the strict economy of motion that comes only after many years on the water, and yet the line shot out in front of him for forty feet or more and the flies settled lightly on the surface of the pool.

He let the flies drift downstream on their own, but he watched the little orange indicator like a hawk. Nothing. When he judged that the flies had reached the deepest holding water in the pool, he pulled a foot of line through the snake guides and twitched the flies with the rod. The orange dot stabbed quickly down beneath the surface and his right arm came up at the same instant. The line tightened, and little beads of spray were thrown off the leader as a trout began thumping hard down among the stones at the bottom of the pool.

How many times had this scene been played and replayed since that first fly-caught trout, some forty years ago? Thousands, tens of thousands of times, and measured in thousands of miles, driven and walked, from the granite ridges of New England all the way to the misty fjords of Vancouver Island, where he had cast to sea-run cutthroats as gray whales breached and sounded off the rocky headlands, and the wild surf pounded his back as he hauled his line into the blue-green Pacific. In the beginning he had sought to possess trout, but now he realized that it was they who possessed him, that trout were a dream, sometimes a nightmare, and he had chased them for so long that he was utterly lost in that dream, just like his father and his grandfather before him.

Carefully he brought the fish in for release, admiring its clean, bright form and vivid colors for a moment before it squirted away back into the pool. He fished until darkness came on from the east. Woodcock buzzed from the willow thickets as he reeled up for the day, and the first bats of the season flitted about the dim sky as he hiked back downstream to the truck. The warm glow of many lights in many windows shone out into the night as he walked along, and he wondered if the good people of the village knew the power of the wildness that lurked just outside their doors, down by the little creek, or if that was something only an angler would know.

The Black Trout
of English Run

English Run pulls itself together from a series of busy limestone springs that pour out from the base of a tall bluff, somewhere in what used to be called the lead mining district of southwest Wisconsin. The water is clear as air and icy cold in that first half-mile of stream, channeled with watercress and bordered with jewelweed and deep blue forget-me-nots. As the settled hot weather of summer finally reaches Wisconsin, brown trout begin to nose their way up English Run in search of cooler water. One of them survived an attack by a great blue heron to become a legendary fish.

I met the black trout of English Run many seasons ago. It was the middle of a dry, dusty summer when afternoon temperatures routinely hit the century mark in Wisconsin, a state that might see less than two weeks of ninety-degree weather in a normal year. Like many anglers I continued fishing right through the drought, and I began to notice that the search for cool water and trout brought fisherfolk together in ways not seen during a wet year. Herons, osprey, kingfishers, otter, and mink became my daily companions, all of us thrown together in the last shadowy oases where trout could be found.

It was the herons that led me to English Run. Each morning at dawn several birds left a rookery in the sloughs and backwaters of the Wisconsin River and flew north, deep into the hills and valleys of rural Crawford County. With each morning's coffee I studied maps and pondered where the birds might be headed. Then I began hiking the country, working my way into the kind of steep, secluded hollows most people would avoid because of rattlesnakes, naturists, and gun-toting hermits.

One sultry afternoon I was driven to distraction by searing heat, clouds of biting gnats, and thick, nearly impassable stands of stinging nettle. The breaking point came when a squadron of gnats flew into both ears, both nostrils, and both eyes simultaneously. I screamed, inhaling a half-dozen gnats in the process, choked, slapped my face in a futile attempt to exterminate the swarm of bugs, swore, and plunged down a steep slope without any thought for my own safety. A bed of watercress broke my near fall, and the icy water took my breath away as I stumbled into the little stream at the bottom of the hill. Like many Wisconsin spring creeks, English Run is tiny and nearly invisible from the nearest road.

Once I recovered from my baptism in the stream, I began looking for trout. And trout there were, in odd, subtle places: in runnels between beds of watercress, only inches deep; beneath rocks, the fish sometimes turning sideways and undulating to slide beneath the stones; and on top of bare gravel in the riffles, where the broken water alone was enough to scatter a trout's mottled outline and allow it to disappear in plain sight. In an hour I saw enough good trout to wear a smug look. I'd found a tiny stream with good fish in a place that was hell to get to, and I was fairly sure that even the landowner didn't realize its potential.

I was splashing downstream after my reconnaissance when I found the black trout. I tried to use a mat of watercress as a stepping stone, but my foot went right through it. There was a sucking sound like the pop of a cork as I pulled my boot back out, but just before I extracted it I felt the unmistakable bump of a fish. The tangle of cress heaved a little. Then a black torpedo arrowed downstream over the gravel and slid smoothly beneath another cress bed. At first I wasn't sure it was a trout. But when I poked under the watercress with a stick and spooked the fish back upstream, there was no mistaking it. It certainly was a brown trout, and a hook-jawed old brute, too, something over eighteen inches long and by far the best fish I'd seen all day. But it was black, not truly black, but charcoal black over its whole body including the fins, with solid black spots and not a glimmer of red anywhere, quite different from the bright scarlet dots and crimson edges that light up most spring creek trout.

For the month and a half that remained of the trout season I sweated and slithered down to English Run about twice a week, still cursing the heat, the gnats, and the nettles. I caught trout, fine fat trout, especially on weighted scuds and sow bugs dapped along the edges of the cress beds. Bullet-head cricket imitations provoked slashing strikes when floated next to submerged logs or twitched at the bottom of riffles. I got a thick-shouldered fifteen-inch brown that jumped wildly when it felt the steel and landed flopping on the bank instead of the water. But the black trout still eluded me.

Twice a day, two days a week, for six weeks I tried for it. The trout was always in the same place, finning placidly just under the cress bed where I'd spooked it the first time. It seemed detached, even listless compared with the other trout in the stream. I never saw it rise or root for scuds and caddis larvae along the bottom. I could crouch down directly to one side of the trout and watch it for minutes at a time. I could even stand boldly on the bank, fully revealed to the fish at a distance of six or eight feet, and still it wouldn't spook or bolt downstream unless I kicked up ripples by wading. The first day I tried a Hare's Ear Scud fished upstream, and then a tiny Woolly Bugger as I was walking back down. The second day I tried a Shell-back Sow Bug fished upstream and a small Black-nosed Dace streamer downstream. The third day I tried a Pheasant Tail Nymph fished upstream and, in a moment of desperation, a bright orange Mickey Finn cast downstream. Still I got no reaction from the fish. Crickets, 'hoppers, Pass Lakes, Muddlers; short casts, long casts, curve casts, pile casts. Nothing I tried caused even the barest flicker of interest to ripple over the fish where it lay carved in onyx beneath the watercress.

The Black Trout (I'd capitalized him in my mind by now; a sure sign of a deep-seated mania) began to haunt my dreams. I couldn't give up. Every time I fished English Run I tried to catch him, once on the way upstream and again on the way down. And every time I failed.

The maples on the slopes of the steep-walled valley were showing orange highlights and the pastures were yellow with goldenrod as I trekked over to English Run for one last session with the wild spring creek trout. Several of the browns I caught that day blazed with spawning colors, and some of the bigger fish displayed the hooked kypes that mark the male trout during the courting season. But sure enough, when I came around a little bend in the creek, there was the Black Trout, far larger than any fish I'd caught in the stream, laying up beneath the cress bed, still as death, as unperturbed and unimpressed as ever with my fly-fishing skills. There were only a few flies left in my boxes that I hadn't yet shown to the trout, and most of these were big, ugly bass flies that I'd normally have used for smallmouth. With the resignation that comes with the admission of defeat, I cut the leader back to at least 15-pound test monofilament and tied on a multicolored monster of a bass fly. It featured a cupped, spun deer-hair head, rubber legs, and large plastic eyes that rattled like a bag of bones. Slowly and ever so carefully I moved within ten feet of the big brown. The heavily weighted streamer kerplunked into the water about three feet below the Black Trout, and I started stripping in line to effect a noisy, chug-a-chug retrieve that would pull the fly past the trout's toothy maw. English Run exploded.

The Black Trout was not a fish to be taken by conventional methods. As the first ripples of disturbance from the streamer touched its lateral line, the trout whirled around and smashed it fairly, savagely, its scissored jaws snapping for the kill. I've fished for more than forty years, and I have yet to see another trout take a fly as viciously as the Black Trout did when it crashed that streamer. It seemed like all the water would splash out of the creek. Still, it wasn't a fair fight. There was nowhere for the trout to go, and all I had to do was hang on tight and wait until it stopped flopping. It took a few tries, but I finally scooped the fish into my net and waded ashore. The fly had come out during the process, so it wasn't until I tried to lay the twenty-one-inch carbonized beauty on top of the cress bed for a picture that I got a good look at it. What I saw shocked me, and then I understood. What I'd thought were just dark spots or bruises on top of the Black Trout's head were really old heron scars, long since healed. All that was left of the trout's eyes were heavily damaged stumps of tissue at the bottom of mostly empty sockets. It was blind. At last I understood what the Black Trout had been telling me for weeks: that if I keep getting the wrong answer, I should ask a different question.

I held the Black Trout upright in the water by the thick wrist of its tail until it kicked away and glided back to its lair beneath the cress bed. I never saw it again. Sometimes it seems to me that wild trout are so fragile that they don't have much of a future in our all-consuming age. But trout have been honed and hardened by natural selection, asking no quarter and giving none in their endless struggle to survive and reproduce. Given just half a chance, wild trout will improvise, adapt, and overcome many difficulties, sometimes flourishing when we would least expect them to. This is one of many qualities that trout fishers admire and respect in their quarry, one of the mystic cords that bind the spirits of true anglers to the great fish they pursue.

Fishing in Print

Snow is flying with a vengeance today, and school was canceled before I let Onyx out for his morning constitutional. The big black Lab doesn't like to be out in rain or snow. He comes back quickly, snorting, snuffling, and shaking his disapproval of the impertinent weather. We don't know it yet, but more than 120 inches of the white stuff will bury us in Durwards Glen this winter before the April sun finally melts the cold winter away. I dry Onyx off with a thick towel, his favorite part of the proceedings. The colossal dog wiggles and waggles furiously, his otter tail thumping the walls on either side of us like a kettle-drummer. Well, if Teresa wasn't awake before, she is now. I pour a mug of steaming coffee, and the dog and I patter down the hall to the study for a morning of fishing in print.

Arnold Gingrich, fanatic trout fisher and longtime editor of *Esquire* magazine, once wrote that "the best fishing is done not in water, but in print." Personally I wouldn't go so far, but sporting books and magazines have certainly helped me through some tough periods in my life when I couldn't get outdoors anywhere near as often as I wanted to. In my early teens I began collecting and archiving fishing books and periodicals. When I started hunting in my mid-thirties, hunting books and magazines started to join the ranks of fishing books on my sagging shelves. Today my fishing collection has over four hundred titles. More than half are about trout fishing, but all fish species and methods are represented and the geography spans the globe. Supplementing the books are hundreds of pounds of magazines, including a complete run of *Hunting and Fishing* from 1931 and '32, a couple issues of *Sports Afield* and *Field & Stream* from the early 1940s through the late '60s, and back issues of *Fly Fisherman* from the early 1970s. Twenty years of *Gray's Sporting Journal* fill several shelves. A few catalog gems have been preserved too, including a 1976 Herter's catalog, H. L. Leonard catalogs from 1975 and '76, and some of the earliest Thomas & Thomas catalogs. At first my collecting was something to fill the long days between fishing trips, but as the years passed I began to realize that my keen interest in sporting history was influencing my success and enjoyment on the water and in the field.

Imagine that two experienced anglers step into a demanding, technical midwestern spring creek in pursuit of cagy, hard-fished brown trout. The first angler has the benefit of several recent issues of *Fly Fisherman, Fly Rod & Reel,* or the *Drake Magazine* to draw on for guidance, and these are excellent publications that help people catch fish all across America on a wide variety of waters. But the second angler has studied hundreds of sporting books and periodicals that reach all the way back to Roman times. Assuming that both anglers are roughly equal in most other respects, the second angler has quite an edge in terms of experiences to draw upon. Even if both anglers turn out to be equally successful in catching fish, the second will probably have more fun and a greater appreciation for the richness of the fishing experience, because he or she can place what they're doing into a historical context. There is history in rods, lines, leaders, knots, the flies themselves, and all the accoutrements that brand us as anglers. There is history in the way we approach the stream; whether we throw flies upstream, down, or across; how we cast; and what we do when we happen to catch a fish. All of our rituals on the water illustrate the steady evolution of the angler's art over thousands of years.

Once we're in the study, I open the curtains to watch the snow while Onyx curls up in the darkness beneath the massive Arts and Crafts–style desk. I set my coffee down on the blotter and settle into a comfortable leather chair that rolls smoothly over to a glass-fronted Amish bookcase. This is the treasure chest containing the jewels of my collection. I open the case and pull out the oldest fishing book I have, an 1859 edition of *Frank Forester's Fish and Fishing of the United States and British Provinces of North America*, which first appeared in 1849 and went through several reprints. Although not a first edition, my copy is a notable example because it retains its original binding in very good condition. The olive brown cover is embossed and features a gilt still life of a trio of British coarse fish laid out along a grassy bank. "Frank Forester" was the pen name of Henry W. Herbert (1807–58), who was born in the United Kingdom, and the cover art may be an allusion to the author's birthplace.

I open to the frontispiece opposite the title page, which is a black-and-white illustration of a "Great Lakes Maskalonge," a muskellunge, our Wisconsin state fish. I sip my coffee and page through the rest of the book, stopping here and there at a choice passage or illustration. I am struck by a remark on page 297, where the author begins a chapter on striped bass fishing in the Atlantic: "The fly will take them brilliantly, and at the end of three hundred yards of Salmon-line a twelve pound Bass will be found quite sufficient to keep even the most skilful angler's hands as full as he can possibly desire." Modern anglers are often amazed to learn that in-shore fly fishing for marine species like striped bass and bluefish was common by 1850.

This points to one of the great truths about fishing: it's hard to be "first" at anything, except for technological firsts like graphite rods, fluorocarbon monofilament, or large-arbor reels. People have been fishing and innovating, and writing about it, for a *very* long time.

On the table nearest my desk is a little book from the Loeb Classical Library series: Aelian, *On Animals*, vol. 3, books 12–17. This is a translation of a Roman text written by Claudius Aelianus around the year AD 200. In book 15, chapter 1, Aelian writes, "I have heard tell of a way of catching fish in Macedonia," and he goes on to describe what is, unmistakably, fly fishing for trout. There is a river wherein live "fishes of a speckled hue." The fish "eat flies [that] settle on the stream," and "so with the skill of anglers the men circumvent the fish by the following artful contrivance. They wrap the hook in scarlet wool, and to the wool they attach two feathers that grow beneath a cock's wattles and are the colour of wax." A few lines later a trout rises to the fly and is caught. There is some debate among classical scholars about a few of the details in the translation, and much debate about the modern name and location of the stream Aelian called the Astraeus. But any angler who reads the passage today knows instinctively that Aelian was describing fly fishing. It has the ring of truth even after some eighteen centuries.

Outside the snow continues to fall and the white cedars are beginning to sag beneath the weight of it. To judge by his twitching paws and wrinkling nose, Onyx is dreaming of pheasants. Wisps of steam rise from my coffee as I massage Onyx's shoulders and reflect on the importance of place for writers and artists.

Wisconsin is well known among hunters, anglers, and conservationists not only for its fish and game opportunities but also for its outdoor writers. Gordon MacQuarrie, who was on the staff of the *Milwaukee Journal* during the 1940s and '50s, was perhaps the first truly professional outdoor writer. John Muir immigrated with his parents to a farm near Fountain Lake (now Ennis Lake) near Portage in 1849, and studied at the University of Wisconsin in Madison before traveling west to the Sierras and immortality. Aldo Leopold's *A Sand County Almanac* is almost required reading for anyone who truly cares about nature and wild country, and the complicated relationship between people, land, and water. The varied physical geography of the Badger State not only has drawn generations of people outdoors, it has inspired them to write about the outdoor experience.

Two old-time Wisconsin outdoor writers who are in danger of being forgotten are Dr. James Henshall, who lived and practiced medicine in Oconomowoc between 1880 and 1910, and Bert Claflin, whose *Blazed Trails for Anglers* appeared in 1949. I have a 1917 reprint of the 1904 revised edition of Henshall's *Book of the Black Bass*. In it, Henshall describes bass fishing with bait, lures, and flies but also includes a whole chapter on "The Philosophy of Angling." Bass, especially smallmouth bass, are at the very top of Henshall's list: "I consider him, inch for inch and pound for pound, the gamest fish that swims. The royal salmon and the lordly trout must yield the palm to a black bass of equal weight." Every summer I fight hordes of black flies to fish a section of the Oconomowoc River that was a favorite of Henshall's. The clear, swift-flowing Oconomowoc looks like a trout stream where it slides beneath a busy highway near the village of Stonebank, but the warm water is home to bluegill, crappie, largemouth and smallmouth bass, rock bass, and several other species that are great fun on a fly rod. Bert Clafflin was one of the first people to write about fly fishing for walleye between 1900 and 1920. The big pool below a dam near Milford, on southern Wisconsin's Crawfish River, was the setting for some of Claflin's happiest and saddest stories.

A sudden clattering in the kitchen tells Onyx that Teresa is up. It's time for him to rouse himself, ruffle-shake, and galumph over to a position where he can snaffle any food item that falls to the floor (or rests on the countertop at what he thinks is too close to the edge). A Lab's cerebral cortex is parceled out like this: ½ hunting, ¼ food, and ¼ sleeping and getting tummy rubs. As Onyx trots out of the room I set down my coffee and survey the rest of my sporting book collection.

When I started collecting fishing books, I searched for titles that I enjoyed reading when I was in my teens without much concern for things like condition, first editions, dust jackets, or authors' signatures.

It was fun browsing the secondhand bookstores in university towns like Madison and Minneapolis–Saint Paul, and every so often I'd find something special. I still enjoy spending an occasional winter afternoon fishing around the dusty shelves of good secondhand bookstores on and off of State Street in Madison. State Street connects the University of Wisconsin on Bascom Hill to the state capitol on the isthmus, and it fairly seethes with intelligent, creative, interesting people all bustling around and bumping into each other like grist in a mill of ideas.

Renaissance Books is a fine store of used and antiquarian books in, of all places, General Mitchell International Airport in Milwaukee. Once, on a chance visit while waiting for a flight to Chicago, I found signed copy number 9 of Charles K. Fox's privately printed edition of the now classic *This Wonderful World of Trout*, which I bought for twenty dollars. On another occasion I chanced upon an 1888 printing of G. Brown Goode's *American Fishes*, intact in its original binding. When I saw the hand-colored illustration of an eastern brook trout on the frontispiece, I simply had to have it whatever the cost.

A few of my books are especially meaningful to me because they belonged to famous angler-authors that I worshiped as a boy. New York's Tony Lyons had family connections to several well-known fly fishers and was a trusted source for these titles. Art Flick was a legendary angler in the Catskill Mountains of the Empire State, and Flick's copy of Brian Clarke's *The Pursuit of Stillwater Trout* now graces my shelves next to an early printing of Flick's own *New Streamside Guide to Naturals and Their Imitations*. It was great fun telling Brian Clarke about this when we fished together on England's River Test in 2004.

Some fishing books I value because they stirred my imagination when I was a kid; Vlad Evanoff's *The Freshwater Fisherman's Bible* and Ray Bergman's *Trout* fall into this category. Others I value for their illustrations as much as for their writing; Larry Koller's *The Treasury of Angling*, Joe Brooks's *Trout Fishing*, Robert Traver's *Anatomy of a Fisherman*, and my complete set of *American Sportsman* hardcover periodicals are examples. For writers, I prefer people like Harry Middleton, Howard T. Walden II, John McDonald, and Ernest Schwiebert. I think Schwiebert's short story "The Platforms of Despair," which appeared in the March 1977 issue of *Fly Fisherman* magazine, ranks as the best fishing story ever written. As you can see, my tastes run to the classics, but I do have a number of fishing books by contemporary authors such as Brian Clarke, John Gierach, Paul Schullery, John Goddard, and James Prosek. The one book that best reflects my own philosophy about fishing and life would be *The Earth Is Enough*, by Harry Middleton.

The books I enjoy most are the ones that I keep coming back to, books full of stories that are almost as much fun to read the fiftieth time around as they were the first time. Of those, there are three that I carry in my truck at all times: *A Summer on the Test,* by John Waller Hills; *A River Never Sleeps*, by Roderick L. Haig-Brown; and *Where the Bright Waters Meet*, by Harry Plunket Greene. These authors assume that fishing is a burning passion for their readers, and they make no apologies for that. They write with humor and grace, and their words echo in my mind as I unhook the fly from the keeper and make the day's first cast.

Anglers Adrift

The three most important things for people who love fishing
are the same three things that make or break a real estate
deal: location, location, and location. Accidents of physical
geography, geology, and climate shape the natural resources of any
landscape. The distribution of natural resources in turn shapes the
human political and economic geography that develops on the land,
and fisherfolk are an inescapable part of that political and economic
geography. Most of us take occasional fishing trips to other places,
but it is our everyday surroundings, our home waters, that mold and
shape us into distinct regional types.

Eons of plate tectonics and continental drift have placed
Wisconsin right in the middle of things. Wisconsin is halfway from
the equator to the North Pole and halfway from the prime meridian
to the International Date Line. Wisconsin was also right in the
middle of the ice age that ended just ten thousand years ago. The
Wisconsin glaciation pushed a lot of rock and dirt around to form
the incredibly diverse natural landscape that we call Wisconsin today.

Six connected fingers of ice a mile thick invaded the Badger State, from the Superior Lobe in the northwest to the Lake Michigan Lobe in the southeast. Although some very interesting landforms, such as eskers, kames, and drumlins, were built near the terminal moraines of the glaciers, their overall effect was to flatten the landscape. When the ice receded, Wisconsin was left with five distinct geographic regions.

The top third of the state from Highway 64 north to Lake Superior is characterized by a thick cover of forest. This is the region Wisconsinites call the North Country, and retreating to a cabin "up north" for vacations is a tradition for many Wisconsin families. The North Country lays claim to Wisconsin's famous trout and smallmouth bass waters, rivers like the Bois Brule, Peshtigo, Saint Croix, and Namekagon. Gordon MacQuarrie's *Stories of the Old Duck Hunters* immortalized these rivers during the middle years of the last century, and one can still hear wild browns slurping mayflies and caddis at night on the Namekagon or see leaping silver steelhead at Rainbow Bend on the Brule. When the dog days of August arrive and trout fishing slows, the smallmouth bass fishing on the Saint Croix and lower Peshtigo rivers reaches a seasonal peak. Northern Wisconsin is lake country too. For many anglers, the rolling boil of a forty-five-inch muskellunge engulfing a surface plug or spinnerbait puts trout fishing to shame. The shallow aquifers feed boiling springs wherever the water table intersects the land surface, which produces a higher density of spring ponds than anywhere else on earth. The increasing popularity of self-propelled pontoon boats and fishing kayaks has led to a trout fishing renaissance on the spring ponds of northern Wisconsin, and some of the best still-water trout anglers in the world live between Langlade and Rhinelander.

Central Wisconsin is a flat expanse of sandy soils that were deposited on the bed of Glacial Lake Wisconsin. This central sands region is trout country too, though increasing demands for drinking and irrigation water have depleted and even dried up several important trout streams in recent years. Sand country streams are typically spring fed and slow flowing. Most of the depth and fish-holding structure is found at the corner bends of rivers like the Pine, Mecan, and White. The western portion of the central sands is cranberry country, and Wisconsin's preferential "Cranberry Law" of 1867 signed the death warrant for several trout streams in this area. We call them cranberry bogs now.

Draw a diagonal line from Janesville northeast to Green Bay, and then widen it to a swath of country about forty miles across and you've encompassed the Rock Valley–Fox Valley corridor. Most Wisconsin residents live here or in Milwaukee County, and like most places the quality of the fishing is inversely proportional to the density of the human population. Several important fishing events take place here, however, including the annual walleye and white bass runs on the lower Wolf River.

Farthest east is the Lake Michigan drainage, where despite the proximity of Milwaukee there is some very good fishing. The Big Lake provides the centerpiece, of course. Four species of trout and two species of Pacific salmon are Lake Michigan's headliners, but there are small but dedicated communities of anglers who target smelt, perch, and other inshore species at certain times of the year. Carp fishing is also beginning to attract a following, especially during the winter months. Smallmouth bass are surprisingly abundant in the Milwaukee River, and there are even small, forgotten native brook trout streams folded secretly into narrow valleys and steep ravines that wend their way through densely populated areas.

So glaciers have made Wisconsin and its anglers what they are. The Superior, Chippewa, Wisconsin Valley, and Langlade Lobes of the ice sheet carved Lake Superior and the North Country, and their interlobate moraines set up the groundwater systems that feed the spring ponds. Glacial Lake Wisconsin gave us the central sands. The Green Bay Lobe shaped the Rock Valley–Fox Valley corridor, and the Lake Michigan Lobe scooped out the basin that became the great lake of the same name. Highway engineers found the level or gently rolling topography and the numerous gravel deposits were perfect for building roads, and all of Wisconsin's interstate highways are sited in glaciated areas.

But a glance at a Wisconsin road map shows an interesting thing. Interstate highways 90 and 94 join together near Madison in south central Wisconsin, but then these main arteries of travel and commerce detour north for many miles before splitting again and turning due west across the prairies of Minnesota and the Dakotas. By doing this the interstates avoid land that the glaciers never touched, a strange land that doesn't quite seem to fit with the rest of the Badger State, even though it conferred the name *badgers* on Welsh and Cornish lead miners who lived there in holes beneath the hills. Residents insist that the region has no mountains, just valleys; places where you can get quite lost on a foggy morning because one valley looks eerily like the next. It is a country of limestone and sandstone bluffs, mysterious caves, trilobites and crinoids, rattlesnakes, jackrabbits, and little rivers that emerge full blown out of the ground. It is trout country, my country. It is the Driftless Area of southwest Wisconsin, and I've roamed and fished and loved it for more than thirty years.

To be fair, the Driftless Area extends into southeast Minnesota and northeast Iowa, but Wisconsin lays claim to most of it. Anglers visiting the region for the first time are struck by the rugged topography of high ridges that suddenly fall away into deep, secluded valleys sometimes called *coulees*. One coworker I took to Timber Coulee for some trout fishing looked around wide-eyed and asked me if we were still in Wisconsin. On misty mornings the Kickapoo Valley looks more like the Appalachians or the Ozarks than the supposedly flat country of the Midwest. This ridge-and-valley landscape markedly affects the pace of life among its residents. Live here awhile and you'll quickly notice that no matter where your destination may be, the road trip will take you an hour or two. A crow has to fly about fifty miles from our home in the Baraboo Hills to Viroqua, but if the crow has to drive my truck he'll log eighty miles if he knows the short cuts.

Residents often define themselves and their families by the valley that they live in rather than the nearest town. People will tell you that they live in Wyoming Valley, Mormon Coulee, Norwegian Hollow, or Durwards Glen. It is essentially a nineteenth-century landscape that has somehow survived into the twenty-first century. When the Civil War began in 1861, most Americans lived on farms or in small towns. In southwestern Wisconsin this is still true, largely because of the inconvenience of narrow winding roads in an area equidistant from Chicago and Minneapolis–Saint Paul. If you want to find the best fishing in the Driftless Area, or indeed anywhere, explore places that are damned inconvenient to get to.

What few straight roads there are tend to follow the tops of the ridges or the floodplains of the larger valleys. Several record floods in recent years have cut people off from the outside world for surprisingly long periods of time. It got so bad in the 1970s that people in Soldiers Grove decided to move the entire town to higher ground, away from the moody Kickapoo River. By 2008 several nearby towns wished they'd done the same thing. For the angler, the straighter roads on the ridge tops are trout alleys. Drive on the high ground along Highways 14, 61, or 18/151, then turn right or left onto a town road or lettered county highway. Within a few miles you'll find yourself driving along a trout stream.

Fishing the Driftless Area means fishing in small or very small streams. There are few natural lakes, and most of them are on the floodplains of the larger rivers. Impoundments behind earthen dams can be found in a few valleys, but agricultural runoff tends to degrade these small reservoirs and the fishing is inconsistent: fantastic in some, mediocre to downright bad in others. Most streams have trout somewhere along their courses. Some streams are dominated by trout but others, especially in the Grant-Platte and Sugar-Pecatonica watersheds, have a mix of smallmouth bass, catfish, walleye, and other warm-water species in their lower reaches. Expect to wade the streams that you're fishing. Wisconsin's Public Trust Doctrine states that anglers may fish navigable streams that cross private land as long as they keep their feet wet. Leaving the stream to go around obstacles, including deep water, is OK as long as you return to the stream immediately by the shortest route.

What makes Driftless Area trout streams special is that they're spring creeks. Spring creeks get most of their water from flowing springs that emerge from limestone bedrock wherever the local surface topography intersects the water table. As a result, a spring creek's volume and temperature stay more constant than freestone streams that get their water primarily from surface runoff. Percolation through limestone formations also raises the pH of the water, and alkaline trout streams support a higher density of aquatic insects, crustaceans, and other trout foods per acre than acidic streams. These factors come together to make spring creeks the premier trout streams in their regions, no matter where on earth they occur. From England's hallowed Rivers Test and Itchen to France's legendary Risle, from Croatia's hauntingly beautiful Gacka to Pennsylvania's historic Letort Spring Run, and west to Montana's Paradise Valley, most world-famous trout streams are spring creeks.

A little quick math shows that southwest Wisconsin boasts 625 spring creeks distributed across fifteen counties, which when added together total an astonishing 2,150 miles of prime trout water. Wild brown trout abound, but native brook trout seem to gain more ground each year and even rainbow trout can be found in some streams. Southwest Wisconsin is also the best place in the world to hunt for tiger trout, a rare and beautiful hybrid produced when a male brook trout spawns with a female brown. Combine attributes like these with inspiring country and you'd think that the Driftless

Area would be a major destination for America's trout anglers. Some folks would like to believe that it could be, but that won't ever happen and I'll tell you why: Wisconsin spring creeks are too darned small. They can be nasty little buggers to fish, especially when the riparian vegetation reaches its late-summer peak and the streams get low and clear. As a red-faced, frustrated Montana angler asked me pointedly one hot July afternoon, "What's *big* about the Big Green?" Visiting anglers whose home waters are in America's eastern and western mountains will drive right over a Wisconsin spring creek and never even see it.

So demanding are the spring creeks of southwestern Wisconsin that many resident fly anglers give up and become *casual* fly fishers: people who fish for trout only a few times a year, and usually on more forgiving streams in Wyoming or Montana. But the survivors, hard-core fisherfolk who never give up even years or marriages after they should have, are molded and shaped to fit these maddeningly difficult, heart-breakingly beautiful trout streams. If you know what to look for you can spot a Driftless Area trout hawk every time.

First off, they fish graphite fly rods that have twenty-five-year or lifetime guarantees against breakage, because they know that the game usually requires casting in jungles where bamboo rods fear to tread. I break a fly rod every couple of seasons. The usual scenario involves a battle-wagon brown who lives under a low bridge. A *very* low bridge; in fact, the lower and snaggier the bridge, the bigger the trout will be. This may require some creeping and crawling so that I can get into position for a short cast. Long, lyrical casts on small, overgrown spring creeks keep a lot of professional fly tiers in business.

Finally I'm in position and the big brown is still on station. Sadly, I now realize that the foliage I've been cheek-by-jowl with for the past thirty yards is rife with poison ivy and wild parsnip. But no matter; the sole task at hand is to put a fly over the fish. This I do by judiciously employing the signature Badger State cast known as the bow-and-arrow cast. The fly is launched, but the distance is still too great. Give me some cams and a couple of pulleys and I might try a compound bow-and-arrow cast. But on the second try the fly lands true and the trout-of-my-dreams slurps it confidently. Even wily brown trout that live in impossible places can be easy to catch if you can just get a fly or lure (or, heaven forbid, bait) to them somehow. With a practiced flick of my bone-spurred wrist I set the hook and battle is joined. The rod bends into a hula-hoop, and for a few seconds time stands still. Then the hook pulls out, said brown trout disappears beneath a log on the bottom, I fall over backward into the stream, and the rod rebounds upward (smack!) into the concrete above me and breaks neatly six or eight inches below the tip-top. I actually carry my receipts in my fly vest so that I'm prepared if I need to stop by Cabela's in Prairie du Chien to exchange the broken stick for a new one. If any maker of hand-crafted split bamboo fly rods is willing to do the same, including living in Prairie du Chien (loosely translated from the French as "Prairie Dog"), I'd be happy to do all this with a cane rod.

Coulee country anglers wear the cheapest breathable hip waders on the market, the feet of which are firmly laced inside ultralight wading boots. Cheap, because I can unerringly walk plumb-dumb into the only loop of rusty barbed wire sticking out of an anthill in an eighty-acre pasture. I have proved this many times. Torn waders or not, the ultralight boots keep my fifty-year-old legs in the game despite the miles and miles and miles of rough walking that Driftless Area trout fishing demands.

Time and distance mean nothing to trout hawks. I recall a day when my good trout compadre Peter Grimm suggested that we hike smartly into a secluded hollow guarded by rattlesnakes, fish hard until midday, and then hike out in time for lunch at the Unique Cafe in Boscobel. The first part of the plan went well, including a fancy bit of high-stepping over a four-foot timber rattler. It was a miracle that neither of us was bitten. Once we reached the stream and began fishing there was a good mixed hatch of mayflies and caddis, the water level was perfect, and scads of good-sized brown trout were up and feeding aggressively: a rare day when we caught trout at will. Eventually we trudged out of the hollow just in time to see a burning orange sun set behind the bluffs that towered over the Mississippi.

Finally, trout hawks of the coulees wear a variety of funny hats to keep the August sun from burning their ears to tanned leather, and they can rebuild a tree-tangled leader in no time flat. They can tie blood knots in the dark without a flashlight. They relish sarcasm and ironic humor. When faced with a hatch of #32 Cream Midges, they'll likely match it with a #10 Pass Lake or Black Flying Ant on the end of a 3x or 4x tippet. They catch more trout than you can possibly imagine, and they've seen more sunrises and sunsets, more scarlet tanagers and American redstarts, more waterfalls, trilliums, and rainbows than any other folks around.

Tiger of the Valleys

late-summer sun blazed across a clear sky on the day I first encountered a tiger of the valleys. In pastures beside the river a steady, hot wind out of the south scorched the grass and rattled the ranks of tall corn in nearby fields. It was August 11, 1993. Waves of rising air shimmered over the pastures as I trudged back downstream toward the truck and a cool drink at noon. I'd made the predawn drive west to Vernon County's Timber Coulee in search of the steady dry fly action that comes with the "trico" hatch: tiny, white-winged, black-bodied mayflies of the genus *Tricorythodes* that seem to pick the hottest, muggiest weather to emerge from the stream. I'd played a hunch that the tricos would hatch out in force on that searing August morning, and I wasn't disappointed. There were already clouds of mayflies dancing over the cool waters of Timber Coulee when I walked down to the stream at sunrise. So many insects were in the air at once that from a distance they looked like patches of mist or smoke drifting over the stream for hundreds of yards. The wild brown trout of Timber Coulee were rising steadily, taking full advantage of this insect horn of plenty, and I was after the trout with fine tippets and tiny dry flies.

By noon the trico hatch had tapered off and bank-side temperatures were passing the ninety-degree mark. It was time for a lunch break in an air-conditioned diner, up the ridge in Westby or Cashton. But no trout addict can pass by good-looking water without a cast or two; maybe I could draw out something large from one of the many "lunker structures" installed along the banks of Timber Coulee in recent years. So I hiked beside the rushing stream, enjoying the heat of the summer sun on my neck and shoulders in a way that Wisconsinites dream about during January cold spells. But I also stopped here and there to cast a team of weighted nymphs into the bubble lines, drifting the flies deep beneath the cut-banks wherever the creek made a hairpin bend. As the flies swung around one particularly deep, dark corner, my orange indicator vanished suddenly and I struck the solid, thumping weight of a good trout. The fish bored deep in an effort to snag the leader or rub out the fly. I remember it as a very spirited fight, and I was surprised that when I brought the trout to the net it was only about eleven inches long.

The trout was incredibly beautiful, exceptional even among trout, whose beauty of form and color have inspired more writers than any other fish. Waves of bright carmine-red splashed across its sides below the lateral line. Instead of dark spots, this trout sported ovals and curlicues of black and olive along the top of its back. It had the bright white leading edges on the pectoral, ventral, and anal fins so characteristic of wild trout, especially native brook trout, but this fish wasn't a brookie. Nor was it a brown or a rainbow. After a minute or two I had to admit that this was a kind of trout I had never seen before; but then I remembered an entry in *McClane's New Standard Fishing Encyclopedia*, a monstrous reference book that's been a good companion on many a snowbound winter evening. The trout in my net was a tiger trout, the first I'd ever seen in more than twenty years of trout fishing.

A tiger trout is a hybrid resulting from a mating between a female brown trout (*Salmo trutta*) and a male brook trout (*Salvelinus fontinalis*). Interestingly, trying to fertilize a female brook trout's eggs with brown trout milt simply doesn't work. Such hybridization between species that do not belong to the same genus is very rare in nature, and viable offspring from such a cross are rarer still.

Most tiger trout are propagated artificially in hatcheries as a novelty fish. I've seen them on display at trout hatcheries in Pennsylvania and New York. Utah hatcheries produce enough tiger trout to support an extensive reservoir stocking program. Wisconsin hatcheries raised tiger trout for a short time in the 1970s, but all of these domestic tigers were stocked in Lake Michigan. Eventually the program was discontinued because of poor hatch rates. Wisconsin's rugged Driftless Area may be the only region in the United States where wild tiger trout are common enough to give even the casual trout fisher an outside chance of catching one.

If you should happen to catch a tiger trout, consider it an event of nature equivalent to winning the lottery. The probability of a female brown trout and a male brook trout interbreeding in nature is exceedingly low; there isn't that much overlap between the species even if they live in the same stream. Brook trout typically occupy the cold headwaters of a river system while brown trout predominate in the warmer water downstream. Both species are fall spawners, however, so if there's significant natural reproduction in a trout stream that has both brook and brown trout, there's at least a chance that a few tigers will be produced each season.

But the odds against catching a tiger trout don't end there. Only 35 percent of the young tigers that hatch successfully grow and mature into adult fish, even within the safe confines of a hatchery, because of genetic diseases inherent in the hybrid sac-fry. Tigers that do mature tend to be more aggressive feeders than either brook trout or browns. As a result, tiger trout are relatively easy to catch and offer a high rate of return when stocked in streams, lakes, and reservoirs.

That first tiger from Timber Coulee was the last one I saw for another decade, but I'm happy to report that I've been catching many more tiger trout from Wisconsin's Driftless Area spring creeks in recent seasons. The year 2003 was a red-letter trout season, in part because I caught two tigers, one from a Grant County stream and another in Crawford County. Surprisingly, 2004 rewarded me with four more tiger trout, two from Vernon County and one each from Pierce and Richland counties. Things are definitely looking up for the Wisconsin trout angler who wants to go tiger hunting! All of these recent tiger trout were caught from different streams, but always from stretches inhabited by good numbers of brook and brown trout.

Recent conversations with former DNR fisheries personnel Roger Kerr and Dave Vetrano about tiger trout in the Driftless Area agree with my own experiences. Roger recalls turning up no more than a half-dozen tigers in twenty years of stream surveys, and usually that meant just a single tiger trout in a stream with thousands of brook trout and browns. However, both Roger and Dave have seen tiger trout become more numerous in recent years. As brook trout continue to make a comeback in many southwestern Wisconsin watersheds, tiger trout have gone from being "exceedingly rare" to "a bit better than rare," according to Dave. His electro-shocking crews now find three or four tiger trout each year. Roger characterizes the chance of catching a tiger trout as "about the same as the chance of seeing an albino deer or a doe with antlers." Most of the tiger trout that are turning up in stream surveys are less than a foot long.

Longtime Wisconsin trout angler and guide Bob Wagner once lived along the headwaters of a Richland County trout stream. Bob reported that in 1997 he personally observed a thirteen-inch male brook trout spawning with a twenty-inch female brown trout. In the seasons that followed, Bob caught quite a number of tiger trout in that stretch of the creek, as many as eight in a two-hour session on the water. This is an incredible statistic when compared with states like Pennsylvania, where veteran anglers consider themselves lucky to catch one or two tiger trout in a lifetime.

Some Wisconsin anglers question whether the increased presence of tiger trout is a positive development. Their concern is for the native brook trout and whether the genetics of a wild brook trout population might be "polluted" by nonnative brown trout genes carried by tiger trout. I think that tiger trout are a good thing. They're an indication that brook trout are becoming more numerous in a river system, and that brookies are moving downstream into traditional brown trout areas as the health of a trout stream improves and water temperatures become colder. Since tiger trout are sterile hybrids, there's no chance of genetic pollution by these rare mules of the trout world. More tiger trout in a stream are tangible proof that the quality of trout habitat is getting better and that natural reproduction is taking place.

If a day comes when you catch what appears to be a mutant variety of trout from a stream in the Badger State, take a closer look. Does your trout look more like a brook trout than a brown, and yet it can't be a brookie? Are there twists and turns of mottled olive markings edged in black on the trout's back? Did the trout hit aggressively and fight like a demon before you brought it to your net? Then take a second look at that trout, and maybe a third and a fourth. You may have caught a tiger of the valleys, a fish of uncommon beauty as rare as a meteor shower or a display of the northern lights.

Spring Ponds

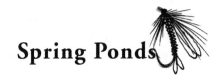

The Scuppernong River has the most unique name in American trout fishing. It begins in several large springs that pour out from the base of an interlobate moraine in southwestern Waukesha County, just twenty miles west of Milwaukee as the crow flies. Spread out a topographic map of the area and you'll easily find the moraine, because most of it lies within the boundaries of the Kettle Moraine State Forest. Trace the line of the moraine south and west to the little village of Eagle and you'll have moved your finger along the divide between the Scuppernong River and Fox River watersheds. As a trout angler, you'll also have noticed a cluster of trout waters in the area, which might be a surprise so close to a major city. Small trout streams like Genesee Creek and Jericho Creek meander south and east from the moraine until they lose themselves in the Fox River, which crosses the state line into Illinois. These streams are well known locally and have a strong following of anglers, some of whose families have fished them for generations. Several large springs drain west from the moraine into the various branches of the Scuppernong. Many of these springs feature spring ponds: Paradise Springs, Scuppernong Springs, McEwan Springs, and McClintock Springs, to name a few. Because a large part of its landscape has been shaped by continental glaciers, Wisconsin is blessed with at least 278 named spring ponds spread across twenty-four counties, a higher density of this special water type than anywhere else on earth. Unique fishing environments tend to produce distinct regional styles among anglers, and Wisconsin is no exception. Fishing spring ponds here has been refined into an art form.

The earliest photograph I have of me fishing was taken on a private spring pond in Langlade County one sunny summer morning in 1966. It shows a towhead kid not quite six years old casting a spinning rod rigged with a nightcrawler and a bobber. The fixed gaze and intense concentration on the kid's face show two things: (1) he's there to *catch fish*, not just play around on the dock; and (2) his life is already ruined. I can even remember details. The rod in my hand is a nifty 5-foot Garcia ultralight with a Mitchell 308 reel on it. If that doesn't work, I've got a heavier 6½-foot Shakespeare "Wonderod" with a Mitchell 300 laid out on the dock within easy reach of where I'm standing.

Despite my best efforts, the only fish I remember catching from this pond were creek chubs. My dad and my cousin had some better days on it from time to time though. In his freezer, my cousin always seemed to have a couple of orange-bellied brookies that were eighteen to twenty-four inches long, and in the late '60s he often won the local *Field & Stream* big fish contest with brook trout from his pond.

In fact, the fishing was so good that he wanted to make more spring ponds from the seeps and tiny streams on his property, and therein lies a story. I can tell it now because the principal folks involved are all dead, and the land changed ownership several years ago.

Somehow my cousin was able to come by some dynamite. Looking back, and I still have some old family photos of the event, it must have been quite a bit of dynamite. At any rate, my dad, several cousins, and some friends who were ex-military types strategically placed the dynamite in an area where the ground was boggy with spring seeps. Somebody lit the fuse and they all ran for the hills. Wives, kids, dogs, et cetera were already on top of one of those hills, the better part of a mile away, with cameras, tripods, and such set up like Cape Canaveral. I remember our blue 1958 Chevrolet Impala flying down the two-rut "road" at the base of the hill, and then my dad and the rest of the guys running to the top and lighting cigarettes. We waited. And waited. Legal niceties weren't discussed by any of the adults present. When I was five years old I just figured my folks knew what the hell they were doing.

Then like a silent movie a vast pillar of Antigo silt loam, black as sin, vaulted into the sky and hung there for a long moment before crashing back down amid the popple and birch. A mighty, booming roar like thunder followed several seconds later. Then all was quiet and people started breathing again. The dogs, however, were convinced that the world was coming to an end and refused to budge from beneath the '58 Chevy. Years later my dad told me he saw forty-foot aspen trees completely covered with mud around the blast zone. We do learn from whatever doesn't kill us though; my cousin built the rest of his ponds with a bulldozer.

I started fly fishing Wisconsin's spring ponds during my undergraduate years at Northland College in Ashland. The headwaters of the White River on the old Henry Ford estate had some nice ones, and I still think of the Delta-Drummond Road through the Chequamegon National Forest as "Trout Alley." Beaver Lake, Nymphia Lake, and Perch Lake were good to me in those early years despite my lack of experience and limited opportunities to fish.

The spring pond I've come to know best is the one I've fished several days each year since it opened to the public in 1985: Paradise Springs Pond, near the village of Eagle in Waukesha County. The spring at the head of the pond flows at a constant rate of about five hundred gallons per minute, or some thirty thousand gallons per hour, making it one of the largest springs in a region where springs and artesian wells are common. European settlers used Paradise Springs (also called Minnehaha Springs or Eagle Rock Springs) as a source of drinking water since at least the 1840s. Trout were stocked in the pond by L. D. Nichols shortly after 1900, although it isn't clear if native brook trout were already present or no trout lived in the pond prior to this initial stocking. Nichols dammed the outlet of Paradise Springs and built a water-driven turbine to generate electricity for his house and grounds, one of the first electrified homes in the area. Trout continued to be stocked by multimillionaire Louis J. Petit when he purchased the property sometime before 1920. Petit, known as the Salt King because he made his fortune with Morton Salt, built a horse track, a tennis and shuffleboard court, and a beautiful field-stone springhouse featuring a domed copper roof. Nichols's dam is still in place, as is Petit's springhouse. The copper roof lasted until about 1970, but has since been removed.

Paradise Springs changed ownership several times after Petit's death in 1932. Augie Pabst (yes, of Pabst Blue Ribbon fame) inherited the property from Petit and sold it to a gentleman named Frank Fulton just after World War II. The paperwork barely had time to dry before Fulton sold the works to Gordon Mertens. Mertens built the Paradise Springs Hotel in 1948, but business must not have been too good because the hotel was transformed into a bottling plant during the 1950s. Lullaby Baby Drinking Water was marketed throughout the region until the bottling plant closed ten years later. The building was removed in the 1970s when the State of Wisconsin acquired the property, and with the help of the local Lions Club, Paradise Springs was restored to its present condition. The Southeast Wisconsin chapter of Trout Unlimited has also done good work at Paradise Springs in recent years, stabilizing the banks and keeping the pond accessible to anglers, including those who get around with wheelchairs.

I didn't know about the spring pond the first time I fished there. February 23, 1985, was a dim, overcast winter's day, but I'd read in the trout regulations that Paradise Springs *Creek* was open for catch-and-release fishing upstream from County Highway N north of Eagle. When I arrived at the now-familiar parking area shortly after dawn, my heart sank. The creek was microscopic, and chock-full of downed trees. But I'd come fifty miles to fish, so with what I call grim determination and Teresa calls sheer cussedness, I tied a #14 Gold-ribbed Hare's Ear Nymph to the tippet and waded into the stream just above the culvert where it flowed beneath Highway N. Nothing happened as I worked my way upstream beneath giant oaks, Norway spruce, and scotch pine, but I kept going and cast wherever I could to wherever a trout might hold in that tiny creek. The unmistakable sound of falling water grew louder as I fished upstream, and finally I came around a bend and saw the tall spillway of Nichols's dam ahead of me. Climbing up the dam from below was a bit of a trick given the ice, snow, and frozen ground, but I was a lot younger then.

Sure enough, a beautiful spring pond opened her arms to greet me as I came over the rise. I can still see it in my mind's eye: a smooth expanse of blue-green water stretching a hundred yards ahead, with the barren, dripping trees and low clouds reflected in it like Japanese calligraphy on parchment. Then a fish broke the surface only fifteen feet away, and I flipped the little nymph into the pond a few feet off to the side of the rise. The hare's ear sank immediately and I watched as the leader pulled under, bit by bit. There was a sudden acceleration in the sink rate, I struck, and a fat nine-inch brown trout leaped into the air, head shaking and body twisting, the first of a dozen fine trout I caught before reeling up at noon.

I had the pond to myself that rainy Saturday morning, something unheard of nowadays. Square wooden cribs of crossed timbers had been placed in some of the deeper areas to provide structure for fish and homes for invertebrates. Scuds and sow bugs grazed in the weed beds, and once I saw several trout following a silver-coated muskrat as it swam through the weeds. The fish were snapping up crustaceans and olive mayfly nymphs dislodged by the muskrat. I stayed with the Hare's Ear Nymph, fishing it deeply with a slow, hand-twist retrieve, watching the line and feeling for strikes.

With Polaroids I was able to sight-fish, and all of my best trout were taken this way rather than fishing the water blindly. Once I cast the little nymph two feet to one side of a crib and watched intently as the fly sank toward the bottom. I quickly lost sight of it, but my eyes bored holes in the water where I knew the nymph must be, and that sixth sense common to all anglers warned me of impending drama. Sure enough, a dark form cruised out from the crib and stopped suddenly. I struck, and a moss-backed brook trout as large as any I'd ever seen writhed savagely in the green deeps, open mouthed, it's head shaking wildly from side to side. I gave a sigh of relief when it finally sagged into the net, fifteen inches and two fat pounds of stunning Wisconsin brook trout. Then I removed the fly, held the big brookie upright in the water, and admired it for several long seconds before it swam away and vanished into history. Lesson learned: when sight-fishing nymphs to trout in still water, watch the fish and not the fly. Strike hard and fast when the trout slows down or stops moving. This also illustrated the primary difference between fishing a stream versus fishing a pond for trout. In a stream, most trout stay in one place while the moving water brings food to them. In a spring pond, most water stays in one place while the trout move around to find food. If an angler can get into the right position on a pond or lake and stay there, cruising trout will swim past every few minutes for as long as the person wants to fish.

At that time the banks around the northeast side of Paradise Springs were reinforced with corrugated metal flashing wired to steel posts. There was a clear space between the flashing and the first weed beds about three feet out from shore, then more clear water on the farther side of the weed beds. Obviously trout should have been cruising and feeding along the outer edge of the weed beds, and I did catch several gorgeous brookies from the pond side of the weeds. But I had a nagging feeling that I ought to be fishing the bank side too, and finally I did send a cast about thirty feet ahead that settled the nymph within a foot of the metal flashing, in mere inches of water. For a moment I could see the dark Hare's Ear Nymph resting on a patch of sandy bottom. Then a sixteen-inch brown trout suddenly swam into view and vacuumed up the fly. I saw little puffs of sand and silt blow out of the trout's gills just before I set the hook. Minutes later, two pounds of copper-colored, red-spotted brown trout shook its head in a mixture of fright and indignation as it swam away after release. Lesson learned: Even in deep spring ponds, trout food is concentrated in the shallower areas not far from the bank. Go slowly, search the shallows intently, and don't be too surprised to see large trout foraging in water barely deep enough to cover their dorsal fins. My bird-hunting mentor Peter Grimm applied this lesson while fishing Paradise Springs in early March 2005. The brown trout that inhaled his #16 Pheasant Tail Nymph was twenty-five inches long. He laid it out on the snow and measured it.

That's the primary attraction of still-water trout fishing; trout in lakes and ponds commonly attain dimensions rarely seen in streams. And in ponds these giants are fishable and catchable during the day, while trophy trout in streams are often holed up beneath log jams where no fly, bait, or lure can reach them or they feed actively only in the middle of the night. Having read this far, you might think that every spring pond in Wisconsin must be dotted with anglers every day of the season. Not so, and I'll tell you why: spring ponds are notorious for their difficult fishing. Many expert trout anglers, especially fly fishers, have come away from a session on a pond or lake with deflated egos and humble hearts. I've even seen them look around self-consciously while walking out, to see if anybody was watching. One mild January morning this season I saw eight different anglers trudge down the snow-covered path to fish Paradise Springs. Two stayed for less than an hour; the others fished patiently for several hours in a stiff wind and temperatures well below freezing. A grand total of one trout was caught and released.

The difficulties begin with access. Most anglers who attempt to wade a Wisconsin spring pond vanish without a trace into the light calcareous ooze, called *marl*, that covers the bottom. I sometimes think that archeologists of the future will scratch their heads and wonder what led us to sacrifice so many fly flingers in the style of the Mayan cenotes. Float tubes are another potential death trap. Rhinelander's Jon Kort, widely acknowledged as the "Lefty Kreh of the spring ponds," once had to rescue an angler whose legs became stuck in a mixture of marl and weeds. Sunk deep in the frigid water in light, breathable waders, unable to move legs numbed by cold, the trapped fly fisher was lucky he didn't die of hypothermia before Jon found him. Use a pontoon boat, kayak, or a canoe to fish a spring pond in style and safety. It's a good idea to fish a remote spring pond with a buddy.

Trout in still waters generally have plenty of food, so they're in no rush to commit fishy suicide by taking your fly. Exasperatingly picky trout that sometimes look closely at *natural* flies before taking them are the norm. It gets even worse on catch-and-release ponds like Paradise Springs, or ponds that hold mostly brown trout. Be patient and persevere or skedaddle to the nearest golf course. Heck, I'd be a lot happier if more anglers *would* stop cluttering up the trout waters in my bailiwick and take up golf instead! Bridge is a lot of fun too, so you might try that as an alternative to not catching trout in spring ponds.

The Four-Minute Fly Tier

The golden sun of a late August afternoon is slanting through the tall hardwoods and pines on the west side of our property as I pull my fly vest out of the truck. The long meadow stretches of the Big Green River are on my mind for tomorrow. The Big Green runs ice-cold even during late summer heat waves, and it's been awhile since I've fished over that way. One by one the fly boxes come out, are examined, and then put away again once I've made mental notes about what patterns and sizes I'll be likely to need for this trip. August is cricket time in Wisconsin and September is grasshopper time. I'm happy to see plenty of these big terrestrial dry flies lined up in rows and ready to be knotted to the end of a stout leader. The lid of my main dry fly box closes with a satisfying snap and I zip it back inside its pocket. But when I look over my nymph box I find that the ranks of flies have thinned quite a bit since the beginning of the season. Some patterns are represented by just a couple of well-chewed, scruffy characters. I'll have some work to do this evening.

Once back inside the house I head downstairs to the familiar corner of our basement that is devoted to fly making. This corner gets thoroughly cleaned about once a year, in October or November once the trout season is over and hunting is in full swing. There's so much involved with getting ready to hunt, hunting, and the aftermath that I don't usually start tying flies again until late December or early January. Then the clutter gradually builds in that special corner of the basement until a seasonal peak is reached in late August or early September. By then it is what Teresa calls "a sight," as in "Don't you dare let anyone see our basement—it is *a sight*!" I switch on the fluorescent light over the fly-tying desk and a pleasant confusion of feathers, fur, hair, synthetics, hooks, tools, boxes, and other paraphernalia of the fly tier's craft comes into view.

I started making my own flies at about the same time I started fly fishing in the mid-1970s. In the beginning it was a question of economy. There was no way I could afford to buy enough flies on an allowance and paper route money. Prices for flies in the 1977 Orvis catalog ranged from seventy cents apiece for traditional wet flies to more than two dollars each for some Atlantic salmon patterns. Standard dry flies were ninety cents each, and nymphs cost eighty cents each. Converting these prices into today's dollars using the Consumer Price Index shows what I was up against. That #16 Adams dry fly that sold for ninety cents in 1977 would be like paying more than three dollars today. Amazingly, the math shows that flies were a lot more expensive in the 1970s than they are now.

Fly acquisition was one thing; fly attrition was, and still is, another. If the fate of most flies was to be cut to ribbons by trout teeth, none of us would complain. But the hard truth is that most flies used on Wisconsin's trout streams end up in trees—fly-eating trees. Some fly-eating trees on our larger spring creeks have become famous among anglers. These foul, despicable, evil dendrites are cunningly placed just where one's last false cast needs to go in order to land the fly on the sweet spot of a particular pool or run. The demise of many small dairy farms, with their herds of tree-eating heifers, has led to good times for fly-eating trees and shrubs along Wisconsin's trout streams.

Trees may be the biggest offenders but there are many other ways to lose flies. Ever drop your last #28 Trico Spinner or Griffith's Gnat while the trout were slurping midges all around you? I recall a day on the west fork of the Kickapoo when I saw Peter Grimm apparently kneeling in prayer behind the tailgate of my truck. Knowing Pete to be a devout soul, I wondered if it was a holy day of obligation. But no; when I reached the truck I learned that he'd dropped his last Pheasant Tail Nymph right there along the shoulder of the road. Both of us bored holes in two square feet of gravel with our eyes for ten minutes without finding it. Now I carry a small but powerful shop magnet mounted on a telescoping handle for use in these situations. If the fly is in anything from bare ground to low grass, a few sweeps with the magnet usually recover it. Sometimes the magnet comes back with several flies, only one of which is mine.

I've lost several fly boxes over the years, and each and every one was a heart-breaker if not a wallet-breaker. The first fly box I lost was a Perrine aluminum box stuffed to the gills with dozens of flies that

Granddad gave me once he realized that my passion for trout fishing wasn't going to fade away. It bounced out of a bicycle pannier that I'd forgotten to zip shut during a long summer ride to an Illinois pond. I searched the shoulder of that road in the hot sun for several days trying to recover it, but to no avail. And just this season I lost my main nymph box somewhere along the Rush River during my annual trip to fish the sulphur hatch. It made me sick to think of the hours and days of work that went into filling that box with enough flies to get me through most of the season. The memory of seeing my vest pocket yawning empty and unzipped is still crystal clear and pathetically sad. What's more, I guarantee that it will happen again. When fishing, the excitement and thrill of the moment are just as intense for me now as they were when I was a kid, and in that excitement I can forget a lot of mundane things such as making sure that zippered pockets are zipped shut.

Given the twin challenges of fly acquisition and attrition, it was clear to me that I was going to have to be able to make my own flies if I wanted to fly fish at all. When I saw a generic fly tying kit for sale at a local sporting goods store for about ten dollars, I bought it as soon as I could scrape up the cash. The materials in the kit were short on quality but long on bright colors. There were several dyed chicken necks, chenille, tinsel, hooks, a couple of spools of tying thread, a cake of wax, several squares of various animal hides, and a little vise made from two pieces of tool steel and two screws—one large screw to hold the vise to the tying desk or table and another, smaller screw to hold the hook between the jaws of the vise.

No one we knew tied flies, so I learned from books. Jim

Quick's *Trout Fishing and Trout Flies* (Countryman Press, 1957) was one reference I consulted often. The Orvis catalog was another. I wondered why the folks at Orvis would print such detailed photos of flies they were trying to sell. It seemed to me that people would just sit down at their tying benches and make copies of the flies that they wanted rather than pay top dollar for them. When I sat down at my own bench to do just that, I soon decided that no one who could afford to buy flies would ever submit to the torture of making his own.

Just getting my vise to hold the hook firmly was a major issue, and I had to use pliers to solve the problem. I didn't have a bobbin, so I used a long piece of thread and tied a half-hitch after every tying operation. I still use half-hitches even though it's something many tiers disapprove of. With today's tying threads, *one* half-hitch after every step in the tying process doesn't visibly increase the bulk of a fly and it greatly increases durability. For some reason I found dubbed fur bodies to be especially difficult when I was learning to tie flies, and it was years before I could spin a decent body of fox, muskrat, or hare's mask on a trout fly.

Fortunately the bass, sunfish, and crappies in Illinois farm ponds weren't very selective, and my cobbled-together flies caught a lot of fish. Usually I didn't fish for trout more than fifteen days a season, so I could buy a few bona fide trout flies occasionally and save them for days when I was actually trout fishing. Looking back over my journals, I find that it took about ten years before I was confident that the trout flies I made myself were as good as or better than those I bought in sporting goods stores, or from the Orvis and Herter's catalogs.

Having to work from pictures and never having set foot in a bona fide fly shop, I usually just tried to make a fly that resembled what I saw in the picture. Stacking, spinning, and clipping deer hair was far beyond my skill level in those first few years, and anyway I didn't have the faintest notion that was how flies like the famous Muddler Minnow were tied. My faux Muddler Minnows had heads built up with layers of light brown chenille instead. These faux Muddlers did yeoman service on many a hot summer evening on the big Delaware in Pennsylvania. I have great memories of chunky bronze-backs hammering the flies and tail-walking across the darkening rapids as the sun set behind the Delaware Water Gap and the mist began to rise. Then again the neat, aesthetically built Muddler Minnows in the Dan Bailey catalogs were really quite different from the original pattern. Canadian Don Gapen's first edition of the Muddler was rough and unprofessional by today's standards, but there was no doubt about its ability to catch fish from the very beginning. Smallmouth bass still can't resist one if it comes swinging along the bottom of a riffle or run.

I'd never seen a genuine blue dun hackle cape and couldn't have afforded one anyway, so my Quill Gordon and Catskill-style wet flies sported sky-blue hackles taken from a Herter's dyed rooster neck ($1.87 in 3A Grade, 1976 catalog). Nevertheless, my true blue Quill Gordons filled a number of creels with limits of fat, educated brown trout from flat-water Wisconsin spring creeks near Dodgeville. Those trout should have known better, but I guess they didn't pore over the Herter's catalog every morning at breakfast like I did. A few years later when I finally visited a real fly shop in Wilmette, Illinois, I was rather shocked to see what a real blue dun cape looked like. I immediately forked over just about all of the money I had on hand to buy one. My journals show that the correct Quill Gordons were no more effective in my hands than the Baby-Blue Duns that preceded them, but I felt a lot better about tying the pattern properly. Even then Theodore Gordon was one of my favorite fishing authors, and I wanted to honor his memory by fishing with flies he would have recognized.

From these early experiences I learned one of the great truths about fly tying that some people don't want you to know: a feeding fish that isn't aware of the angler's presence will usually take the first fly that it sees. Bass like a big mouthful, and anything in the strike zone that gives the impression of live food generally results in a take. Ditto for pike and muskies, especially if you trigger their chase response. Brown trout that have a well-deserved reputation for fussiness and selectivity will strike an amazing variety of flies in assorted sizes, shapes, and colors, unless there is such an abundance of one particular food that the fish lock onto that one item exclusively. And even then many successful trout anglers fish a hatch with "cripples," poorly tied flies that suggest a bug with birth defects that can't get away.

There is great satisfaction in crafting a well-tied fly that is nearly perfect in color and proportion, but such quality is more impressive to other fly tiers than it is to fish. Anglers who are just starting out in fly tying should never throw away a fly just because it doesn't look right; just hide it from the instructor and fish it with confidence tomorrow. I say "hide it from the instructor," because some fly-tying instructors in my area have been known to take a single-edged razor blade to the hook of any student whose monstrosities veer away from the standard proportions for that pattern, thus destroying the student's efforts and forcing him or her to start over with a bare hook. Thankfully, fish are much more forgiving than fly-tying instructors.

It took many years before I really began to enjoy the craft of fly tying. Modern threads are much stronger for their diameter than what was available twenty years ago, and this has largely removed the frustration of breaking the tying thread at a critical juncture when tying a fly. Invest some serious money in a top-of-the-line vise once you're sure that the fly-fishing and fly-tying virus has taken hold. I've never regretted the heavy chunk of change that I laid on the counter for my beautifully machined DynaKing, and many experienced tiers are just as happy with their Regals and Renzettis. As in any art or craft, quality tools are a joy to use and they make it much easier to tie flies that you're happy with. It's hard to beat tools designed by the late Frank Matarelli, especially his signature whip-finishing tool for making a small, neat head on a fly. A proper whip finish was something I struggled with for a long time, but Matarelli's tool made it easy. It's funny though; after using the tool for a couple of months, I found I no longer needed it. I could do the same thing with my fingers. So a good whip-finishing tool can function like training wheels on a bicycle.

I think you'll find that under the twin influences of your home waters and your local fly-fishing crowd, your finished flies will have a distinctive regional style. Here in Wisconsin many of us specialize in "throw-away flies" that take only a couple of minutes to tie, again keeping in mind the fly-eating trees and shrubs that infest most of our small trout streams. One of our top local trout guides ties a scud pattern that consists of a lead-wrapped hook covered with dubbing. Superglue is applied to the dorsal surface to form the shell-back, and the fly is finished. Much of his time is spent guiding beginners, many of whom have never cast a fly let alone caught a trout on one. If a client burns through a dozen or three superglue scuds over the course of a day's fishing, who cares? And these flies are deadly effective in skilled hands anywhere on spring creeks where scuds abound. I often trail a scud with a small Sawyer Pheasant Tail Nymph. To craft this pattern I need eight barbs from the tail feather of one of last year's roosters and an eight-inch hank of bright orange wire. That's it. In fact, most of the time Frank Sawyer worked trout magic with just two flies, the aforesaid Pheasant Tail Nymph and a Killer Bug. The Killer Bug, one of the deadliest flies ever devised, is a weighted nymph hook wrapped with gray wool. Old Frank Sawyer was perhaps the finest nymph fisherman in England back in the day, and I'll bet you a fistful of the queen's shillings that the Officers' Association water on the River Avon was rife with fly-eating trees.

Nets

A net is a tangible connection to a time before history and before
written language, a time when fishing and hunting *were*
life in a direct visceral way. Thirty thousand years ago,
when our ancestors began drawing images of the Pleistocene world
and the great beasts that lived in it on the walls of caves, they fished
with nets. Net making is an ancient craft practiced by many people
even today. Once while attending a conclave of fly fishers in northern
Wisconsin, I saw net maker Karen Passmore quietly take a seat in the
back row just before the feature presentation. As the presentation
about fishing for trout in spring ponds began, Karen brought out her
simple tools and cotton cord and began weaving a net. She never said
a word, but by the end of the presentation there was a ring of people
gathered around Karen, watching as she worked her magic.

The first nets I used belonged to my grandfather. Somehow the
Pleistocene gene skipped a generation in our family. Granddad hunted
and fished every chance he got, but Dad hunted only occasionally
when I was small and never after I was about ten years old. My dad

was one of those poor devils who never should have fished either. He had a lethal combination of cerebral gunpowder coupled with an abiding impatience connected to an embarrassingly short fuse. After being stuck in the same boat with Dad during a couple of blowups, it occurred to me that I needed to do three things: (1) fish in a way that he didn't, thus minimizing our time together on the water; (2) when fishing, fish as far away from him as possible; and (3) not go anywhere near his gear and tackle when he was around. Granddad knew perfectly well what was going on and quietly made it possible for me to do all three things.

My grandfather was a big, kind man whose piercing blue eyes were lined with crow's feet from smiling too much. He lived in Nazareth, Pennsylvania, within easy biking distance of the Bushkill, a typical eastern freestone trout stream. He encouraged me to go fishing as often as I liked, and he let me borrow whatever fishing gear I needed. When he had time, we would drive to some great trout streams in the Pocono Mountains or to the Delaware River for smallmouth bass. The summers I was able to spend with my grandparents were golden.

Granddad had two nets that hung from a nail on the wall of his garage. The first was a rusty, spring-steel, collapsible frame model that I never actually saw him use. The second had a white ash frame weathered to a golden patina after many years of hard use and a cord-wrapped handle. This net captured a four-pound Delaware River smallmouth for me when I was eleven years old, and it was the one I took trout fishing with me during my teenage years.

The summer that Granddad died, Grandma gave away almost all of his fishing gear and sold his garage full of woodworking tools as scrap. I remember how my heart sank when I drove out to see her that August and opened the garage door to emptiness. The only piece of fishing tackle left in the garage was the ugly duckling steel net that Granddad almost never used and nobody else wanted. That net now hangs from a nail in my garage. I never use it either, but whenever I take it down from its place of honor to look at it, happy memories of long ago fishing days come back to me as fresh as this morning's rain.

During my years as a journeyman fly fisher in southern Wisconsin I went through a series of production model nets sold through the two major sporting supply houses, Gander Mountain and Cabela's. It took me quite awhile to realize that the device, more properly called a release, that attaches the net to the wading angler is just as important as the net itself. A loop of elastic slung over the shoulder sufficed for Granddad's nets. The problem with that system was graphically illustrated one day when I was fishing a small, brushy tributary of the Bushkill. The net snagged on some blackberry canes as I walked along the bank. I was scanning the water ahead for fish when the net broke free of the blackberries and catapulted into my back with so much force that I was afraid I'd lacerated a kidney. After that episode I cut off the elastic and attached an elegant piece of metal called a French clip instead. The French clip was an improvement, but the contortions required to release the net from the back of my fly vest made me wish I was an octopus. Now all of my nets have a Rose Creek release affixed to them, and this system of Delrin snap clips seems to be the last word in net releases.

In any event, I didn't carry a net very often during my first years as a fly fisher. It was worth the hassle only on days when there was a fair chance of catching an exceptionally large fish. Because I didn't carry a net every time I went out, there were several occasions where I lost my net in happy ignorance, not remembering that I'd taken it with me until hours, even days later when I couldn't find the darned thing.

I recall a perfect June day on the west fork of the Kickapoo River above Avalanche. Puffy cumulus clouds drifted across a wide blue sky, temperatures settled somewhere in the midseventies with a light breeze out of the northwest, and trout, even big trout, were on the prowl. I got to the Volkswagen hole (named for a junked VW Beetle parked in its final resting place beside the river), unhooked my nymphs from the keeper, and began sending long casts toward the fast water at the head of the pool. During one of the drifts, my indicator took a little hop and I struck the solid, thumping weight of a good trout. 'Round and 'round the pool we went, but I finally breathed a sigh of relief when the thick-bodied seventeen-inch brown trout sank into the fine mesh of my custom-made cherry-wood trout net. For a few minutes I sat on the bank and admired the beautiful trout as it lay inside the net, now sunk in the clear water of the west fork. Then I gently lifted it out of the net and back into the river. Its black-spotted form glided smoothly across the pool on a wide arc into deeper water.

It was only when I got back to the car at lunchtime that I realized I no longer had my net with me. The Volkswagen hole was a full mile downstream through the broad pastures of Amish farms that border that part of the west fork, but downstream I hiked, looking carefully at every fence-crossing but knowing I'd probably left the net on the bank of the pool where I'd taken the big brown. When I got to the Volkswagen hole there were two local kids fishing it with worms. In reply to the age-old angler's greeting, "Any luck?" they replied with a decided negative. "But look; we found this great net just laying on the bank." The kids were really happy and excited about their find, which was likely to be their only catch of the day. For a moment I thought about reclaiming my net, but then I thought, "Oh, hell . . . ," and let them have it without letting on that it was mine. This has become a recurring theme in my experiences with nets. Those bought with pieces of silver are eventually lost or given away, but the nets that have come to me on their own, unexpectedly, have stayed with me down the years.

My set of Stoney Creek nets is a case in point. I have three of them. Each frame was handcrafted from richly grained walnut and maple by Dan Passmore of Rhinelander, Wisconsin, and each bag was handwoven by Karen Passmore, Dan's spouse. Stoney Creek nets are the only nets I know of that are completely handmade. Each of my Stoney Creek nets is the first example of its kind and is labeled #001 in India ink at the end of the handle.

They fit neatly inside one another, just like the nested set of cooking pots I use when I'm camping. The largest, the Steelhead model, measures thirty inches from end to end with a twenty-one-inch bow. Next comes the Trout model, twenty inches long with a thirteen-inch bow, and finally the Gimp model, a mere thirteen inches long with an eight-inch bow. The first two of these nets I won in bucket raffles held to raise money for various Trout Unlimited projects in the Badger State. Since I'm one of those people who almost never win anything at raffles, in each case a helpful bystander had to tap me on the shoulder to tell me that I'd won. The tiny Gimp model is a one-and-only that Dan Passmore built at the request of Jon Kort. Every time I see it I think of crook-backed Jon in his pontoon boat, drifting quietly around some spruce-girt malarial bog in Wisconsin's North Country in search of big native squaretails. Jon Kort is the most talented still-water trout fisher I have ever seen and he's widely acknowledged as the authority on fishing spring ponds in Wisconsin.

The greatest net in my collection was forged of steel and aluminum and brass by Hardy Brothers of Alnwick, England, many years ago, and it came to me in a most unexpected way. Teresa and I made a pilgrimage to England and Scotland in the summer of 2004. Along with visits to historic and literary sites, we wanted to fish the rivers where fly fishing as we know and practice it today was born, centuries ago. The weedy River Test where it purls through the village of Stockbridge in Hampshire remains the center of the fly-fishing universe in the hearts and minds of many anglers. The sunny paths along the water meadows beside the Test have been walked by generations of patient fly fishers for at least five hundred years. Trout are relatively easy to see in the broad, smooth currents of the Test; their behavior and reaction to the fly can be observed and studied on long midsummer afternoons. This is the river where Frederic M. Halford and George Selwyn Marryat developed the modern upwinged dry fly and began casting imitations of specific insects to rising trout. This is where G. E. M. Skues began sight-fishing nymph imitations to visible trout that were not rising. The Grosvenor Hotel in Stockbridge is where anglers came together at the end of the day and told their stories.

The friction caused by these chance meetings and informal discussions over a pint of ale started a firestorm of ideas about fly-fishing practices that has continued down the years to our own time.

We stayed a week in Stockbridge and soon settled into the pace of English village life. Rising early each morning, I took a walk down the village high street to greet the river and the fat brown and rainbow trout that rose to flies or grubbed along the bottom for scuds and sow bugs just a few feet from the edge of the pavement.

Duncan Weston, a tall, white-haired giant of a Scot, was assigned to be our guide for the week. We got along famously right from the beginning. As Teresa and I tackled up on our first morning beside the clear-as-air Bullington Stream on the upper Test, Duncan explained the rules of the water to us. "We've been assigned beat number two," he said. In the UK and Europe, a "beat" is a marked stretch of river that has been reserved for the exclusive use of one or more anglers for a set period of time. The beat system spreads people out and keeps them from getting in each other's way. Duncan continued, "Dry fly and nymph only, and the flies must be cast to visible trout." This wasn't much of a restriction on the crystalline Bullington Stream, where trout and grayling could easily be seen from twenty yards away. "Beat number two is small for a full day's fishing, but I checked the log book today and nobody has signed up for beat number one or beat number three, so we might be able to fish those beats after lunch." With some misgivings we showed Duncan our fly boxes, which were filled with typical Wisconsin patterns like the Bead-head Pink Squirrel, Bead-head Woolly Bugger, Bead-head Prince, Bead-head Biot Bug, and Bead-head Pheasant Tail Nymph. Sure enough, Duncan frowned as he scanned the rows of perfectly tied flies. "What do you think?" I asked. "Well, Kev," he replied, "I've seined the chalkstreams and studied their fly life for more than thirty years, and I have yet to see a nymph wearing a brass deep-sea diver's helmet."

I will always remember that first morning's walk along the beautiful channels of the Bullington Stream, floored with golden gravel and bordered with thick emerald masses of cress and water crowfoot. With every trout and every feeding grayling we passed, my heart beat faster. Finally we reached the bottom of beat number two. Trout were rising quietly beneath the low branches of some hawthorn trees on my own bank. Duncan had a look, and I had a look. Then we conferred. "I think they're taking nymphs a few inches beneath the surface," I said. "It's their backs and tails that are coming out of the water when they rise." Duncan smiled, "Ah, right enough. Have ya' got any Pheasant Tail or Greenwell Nymphs not rigged for mine-sweeping?" I did. Once I had a fly on the leader, I got down on my hands and knees and crept and crawled to the edge of the stream about thirty feet below the feeding trout. Duncan smiled again. I had the butt section of the leader treated to float and the tippet treated to sink. Then I took a deep breath and sent the day's first cast looping over the Bullington Stream.

The little Pheasant Tail Nymph settled onto the surface of the water about thirty-five feet away and sank immediately. I watched the floating part of the leader like a hawk. It stopped and pulled upstream, and I set the hook into a fat, high-flying Test trout. "Boy, you are a show-off, aren't ya'?" Duncan laughed. He handed me his net as I brought the trout in. The net was the usual kind seen on the chalkstreams, where the banks are swampy and the trout have to be netted some distance away from where the angler is standing. A hollow, black anodized steel handle, brass collar, and an aluminum frame were folded up tightly. Duncan took the net in hand and gave it a flip of his wrist. Instantly the aluminum frame rotated forward and snapped securely onto the end of the handle. Then Duncan put his foot into the frame and extended the net handle to its full length of four-and-a-half feet. The extended reach of this long net made landing the trout easy.

Teresa took a photo as I released the fire-gilt two-pound brownie back into the icy flow of the Bullington Stream. Then I cleaned Duncan's net by swashing it back and forth in the water and shaking it dry before folding it up and returning it to him. Duncan looked at me in amazement. "In all the years I've been guiding anglers on the chalkstreams, you are the first to clean my net before giving it back to me," he said.

The end of that week-long, week-short friendship was a sad occasion for both of us. We had shared so many moments of victory and defeat on the broad water of the Test and on the smaller, more intimate River Meon southeast of Winchester. On one of our last mornings together Duncan greeted me in the parking lot of the White Hart in Stockbridge. "I have a present for you," he said simply, and then he gave his net to me.

Turning Back the Clock

Would you like to be young again? All of us ponder this question at some point in our adult lives. The best response is probably "Yes, if I could have what I have now and know what I know now." But it seems to me that, of all people, we as twenty-first-century anglers are in the best position to travel back in time and relive some of the events of our fishing youth. How different things would have been if only we could have fished then with the skill and wisdom we have today. Then again, maybe not much would change, given the limits of the tackle and gear we used in those early days and our limited opportunities to fish. At any rate, there came a day when I thought it would be fun to try and turn back the clock, both to answer these questions and to compare fresh-water fly fishing as it was for me in the mid-1970s with how things are in my fly-fishing today.

The rod rack on my basement landing bristles with the latest graphite rods fitted with racy-looking fly, spinning, and casting reels. But in that gleaming array of twenty-first-century tackle there is one outfit that looks as forlorn and out-of-place as Charlie Brown's Christmas tree. It's a green Garcia Conolon "3-star" fiberglass fly rod that was originally eight feet long (now a tad shy of seven feet nine inches), with a Heddon 310 single-action fly reel attached, and it was a Christmas present in 1974. This was the rod and reel that I used to catch my first trout on a fly, and I kept them as a remembrance.

Not much tackle has survived from that period. As a teenager I fished hard on a tight budget, and most items of tackle I had in the 1970s were lost, broken, or worn out and discarded long ago. Only the rod, reel, and an old Perrine aluminum fly box survive, along with my fishing journal for 1975–82 and my first fly vest (vintage 1976 or '77). Every now and then, especially when I'm taking a break from tying flies on a dark winter night, I walk over and pick up my old rod, flex it, spin the reel a few times, and reverently set it back in its place of honor on the rod rack.

My old green fly rod set a record for end-to-end damage that stands to this day. Somehow I kept fishing with it because I never scraped together enough money to replace it. I don't remember when I broke the tip off, but the repair job was simple. I just biked over to the local sporting goods store, bought a replacement spinning rod tip, and glued it onto the end after cutting away the last snake guide and its thread wraps. The next snake guide had only half of the original thread wraps; the lower foot was tied on crudely with peach-colored sewing thread. This must have started to unravel, because at some later time I reinforced it with black electrical tape. Another snake guide was completely rewrapped, this time with blue sewing thread (and not a bad job really). I liked the nickel-silver ferrules, perhaps the only detail this rod shared with fine cane rods of the day. All of the original decals were worn away except for part of the Garcia crest below the stripping guide and three gold stars above the grip. The keeper ring had completely disappeared. A moment of youthful exuberance damaged the end of the down-locking reel seat: I had tried to hurdle a guardrail at the top of a steep bank while hiking back to the car after fishing Pennsylvania's Beltzville Reservoir. This episode destroyed the butt cap, but I jury-rigged a replacement with some kind of plastic weather stripping cut to size and crudely hammered into place where the butt cap used to be. Amazingly, this battered old fly rod still casts a mean line today and I can catch fish with it. But there was a time when my old rod was factory fresh and gleaming.

In my journal there's a picture of me holding the first good fish I caught with the rod: a twenty-one-inch walleye from below Rough River Dam near Leitchfield, Kentucky. The fish struck a #8 Woolly Worm fished deep at the end of a 3x leader and is still the only walleye I've ever caught on a fly. The picture was taken in March 1975, and I'd had the fly rod and reel for less than three months. They looked stunning. All the guides were intact. The light green fiberglass blank contrasted nicely with the dark green wraps, the decals were fresh, the cork of the grip was pale and new, and the green-anodized reel seat glittered in the sunlight. Where could I find my old rod in new or near-new condition?

The answer, like the answers to so many questions, was on my desktop. Simple searches on eBay turned up lightly used examples of my green Garcia fly rod every couple of weeks. The same was true of the Heddon 310 reel. This tackle was inexpensive when it was new, and I probably paid as much for the rod and reel on eBay in 2008 as my dad did at SportMart in 1974, except that a dollar went a lot further in 1974.

It felt like Christmas when the long cardboard tube arrived in the mail. I carefully unpacked my "new" old green fly rod, mounted the reel on it, and laid it out next to the "old" old green fly rod. The differences were so stark that a casual observer might not have believed that they were the same make and model. All the guides and fittings on the new old rod were intact, including the little wire keeper ring above the winding check. Decals, only slightly deteriorated, identified the rod as a model "#8237-A, 8′, DRY FLY ACTION, AFTMA #6 & 7," details I once knew by heart but had forgotten over the years.

In the mid-1970s such fly rods were considered versatile, all-around fly rods for most freshwater fishing. The 5-weight fly rods were light trout rods; 3- and 4-weight rods were just starting to become popular. The majority of trout specialists that I knew used 7½-foot fiberglass or split cane fly rods that carried 5-weight lines for most of their fishing. Longer rods, whether glass or bamboo, weren't very popular then because they were relatively heavy. The introduction of light-weight graphite (carbon fiber) rods completely altered the fishing landscape, and now long rods are back in vogue. The first production graphite fly rods came onto the market in 1973; the Fenwick HMG series. I bought one in 1990 and loved it, but in 1975 such a rod was out of my very limited economic reach.

Cortland 333 fly lines are still on the market today, so it was a simple matter to buy a reasonable facsimile of my 1975 fly line. Like all successful tackle makers, Cortland has continually improved this entry-level fly line. But one thing has stayed the same over the years: the 333 was, and is, a fantastic value. It casts better and lasts longer than many so-called premium fly lines.

"DRY FLY ACTION" gave me a good laugh when I took my new old fly rod out to the side yard for a bit of casting practice. What was a good, stiff, fast-action rod in 1975 was a snail-slow, floppy action compared to today's graphite rods. At first I didn't think I would be able to fish with such a noodle, but once I slowed down my casting stroke it wasn't so bad. Indeed, I could see a definite advantage to the super-soft rod if the conditions forced me to fish with 7x or 8x tippets, and I recalled that I did have a spool of 8x Maxima in my fishing bag during that first year of fly fishing. I thought of the 8x (0.5-pound test) monofilament as my secret weapon for highly educated Pennsylvania trout.

I was surprised by the memories, visions really, that welled up in my mind while I was casting. I recalled a hot July evening on the big Delaware in Pennsylvania, in the fast water above Sandt's Eddy, where a #6 Muddler Minnow slung as far across the river as I could cast caught five fat smallmouth bass from 1½ to 3 pounds. I could feel the rod bend right down to the handle as a red-eyed smallmouth bored deep in a bid to cut the tippet or snag the fly on the rocks. One rainy October morning on northern Michigan's Platte River, I saw a continuous procession of trophy chinook salmon, coho salmon, brown trout, and steelhead pass by in plain sight while I cast yarn flies and literally shook with excitement. I killed five fish that day, and as I trudged back to our campsite in the cedars, my stringer was so heavy with giant trout and salmon that I could hardly keep their tails from dragging on the ground. There was my first trip to northern Manitoba for walleye and northern pike, where one day I tried to catch a pike on a fly in Grass River Provincial Park, and almost did it too. And there was that magical June day when I finally solved the puzzle of fly fishing southwest Wisconsin's spring creeks. Fishing a Quill Gordon wet fly across and downstream on Mill Creek, I creeled a limit of fat, wild brown trout, trout whose flesh cut as red as a sockeye salmon's when I cleaned them by the stream before hiking over the hills back to the car. All of these experiences happened in my first three seasons of hard-core fly fishing, 1975–77, with that green Garcia fly rod.

Thirty-five years have passed since those days, but I still have a lot of fun turning back the clock every so often. I've discovered that time travel is a question of degree. First-degree time travel happens when at some point during a fishing day I cut off the Klinkhammer, Chernobyl Ant, Gummy Minnow, or whatever currently fashionable fly pattern happens to be knotted to the end of my leader and replace it with a #12 March Brown wet fly or McGinty on the point and a #14 Leadwing Coachman or Cowdung on a dropper. I might turn back the clock even further and fish three wet flies at once, across and downstream in the classic style. Do the old methods still work in the highly charged, super-competitive, five-second-attention-span fly-fishing world of today? Do some research (preferably from old magazines), construct your own time machine, and find out. I don't want to ruin your voyage of discovery.

Second-degree time travel happens when I leave my modern fishing gear at home and take my youth outfit to a lake, pond, or stream that I fished as a boy. My youth outfit is a modest collection of old tackle that is as close as possible to the gear I used from 1975–77: eight-foot green fiberglass Garcia fly rod, Heddon 310 fly reel loaded with a few yards of braided Dacron backing and a DT6F line, and a canvas Arcticreel that doubles as a fishing bag to hold a Perrine aluminum fly box, three or four dozen flies limited to patterns and sizes I used then, some tapered nylon leaders, a couple of tippet spools, and a nail clipper for trimming knots. That was all I carried with me on a fishing excursion. What a stark contrast to the bulging-to-the-limit fly vest I wear on the stream today. Life was definitely simpler then, but I would have made it more complicated if I could have.

Using second-degree time travel to reprise some of my fishing life has been interesting and a bit tricky. Tricky because so much of what fishing is about is connected to particular places, and some of the places that I fished as a youth have changed beyond recognition. Wisconsin's Mill Creek is one example. This Iowa County stream took me under her wing that rainy June day in 1977 and taught me how to catch trout from a small spring creek, an environment very different from the large eastern freestone streams where I caught my first trout on flies. A tail-water fishery below Twin Valley Dam, Mill Creek always had a diverse fish population. Along with brown trout

I caught bluegill, crappie, largemouth bass, yellow perch, creek chub, common shiner, and several species of dace. Even my first two muskellunge on flies were caught in this stream, from the plunge pool at the foot of Twin Valley Dam in the early 1980s. Today there are many more homes along the stream, and the new landowners generally aren't as friendly to anglers as the old farmers used to be. The volume of water in the channel of Mill Creek seems to be significantly lower than it was years ago, but whatever the reasons, warm-water fish are still present in numbers but trout are few and far between.

Happily, streams like Wisconsin's Castle Rock Creek and Pennsylvania's Little Lehigh River are much the same today as they were a generation ago. Of course Thomas Wolfe was right; we can never really go home again because we're not the same people we were then. Casting is one example. In 1977 I couldn't cast a measured fifty feet, but today I can easily drill a three-inch target with a fly at sixty feet using my youth outfit. Reading water is another difference. My experiences with electro-shocking streams during my college years completely altered my understanding of where trout will hold in a river, to the point where today people accuse me of "conjuring trout" from empty water. I can easily catch more and larger trout today with my youth outfit than I could thirty-five years ago. Can the *magic* of those early days be recaptured? Again, just try it yourself and see; that's really the only way to learn anything about fishing.

Third-degree time travel happens when I fish historic water with classic tackle as well as classic methods. Now we're in dangerous territory. Third-degree time travel can suck you in and never let you go.

Like many anglers I've accumulated a thicket of fishing rods over the years, but one stands out as the queen of my collection. Unscrew the brass cap on the rod tube and you'll detect the ancient, unmistakable odor of tung-oil varnish as the nickel-silver ends of four sections of split cane fly rod come into view. Gently pull out the rod bag and you'll notice that the original label is still there, hand-written in India ink almost a century ago. The label identifies the vendor as William Mills & Sons of New York City, and the rod as an H. L. Leonard "Tournament," model 51-H, 9 feet long, 5⅛ ounces, and two tips. The rod sections are in beautiful, lightly used original condition and everything is intact right down to the little nickel-silver caps fitted onto the female ferules. The William Mills label, the style of the Leonard logo stamped on the butt-cap, the agate stripping guide, and the lack of intermediate wraps on the rod sections show that the rod was probably built between 1915 and 1925.

This rod means a lot to me because Theodore Gordon had one just like it. Gordon is often called "the father of dry fly fishing in America," and he was one of the founders of the Catskill School of dry fly fishing that evolved on rivers like the Beaverkill, Esopus, and Neversink. In the spring of 1912, a group of Gordon's friends got together with the goal of purchasing the "finest rod that could be bought" and presenting it to him. Gordon later recounted the event in a letter published in the British *Fishing Gazette*: "A number of delightful friends of mine got together recently and decided to send me a splendid 'Leonard' rod, one of the 'Tournament' class. . . . It is a very powerful rod, a duplicate, I understand, of Val Conson's 'little Leonard.' What a lovely thing to do!" Val Conson was the pen name of British angler G. E. M. Skues, who has justly been called "the father of modern nymph fishing." My goal is to take the Leonard on a fly-fishing pilgrimage to the Catskills, fish a Quill Gordon dry fly across the broad pools of the Beaverkill, and then travel to Winchester, England, and use the rod to fish nymphs in the classic style on the River Itchen, Skues's home river. That will be time travel indeed. And if I should not return, then so be it.

Good Days
and Bad Days

To novice anglers it must seem like the experienced people have all the answers, catch scads of fish every time out, and never have a bad day on the water. The truth is that anybody who claims never to have had a bad day on the water lies about other things too. We do tend to dwell on our successes, and so we should. Always make an effort to remember the good times. If you have a rough day fishing, the best thing to do is forget it and go fishing again tomorrow. To prove this in my own case, all I have to do is look through the pages of my journals.

I've kept a fishing journal every year since 1975. My first journals are handwritten, some in stylish cursive writing, but in 1994 I began using a computer to record data about specific fishing days and descriptions of my experiences. My journals now fill a couple of sagging shelves in the basement next to my fly-tying bench, and as you can imagine I have a small mountain of data and information that I can consult during the fishing season, and a treasure trove of memories I can browse through whenever I'm in a reflective mood. Never pass up an opportunity to look through the journals of an experienced angler or hunter. Such a chance doesn't happen very often, if ever. Since as a reader you've stayed with me this far, I've decided to open up Fort Knox and let you take at least a handful of gold dust. Here are a few selections from my journals, which describe many good days and some bad days. The entries may be condensed, but the journaling is copied faithfully with no editing.

10 July 1983, Onion River, Sheboygan County. A certain brush pile in a bend downstream had attracted Teresa's attention as a likely spot when we fished here last week I crept into casting range and side-armed the wet fly [#12 Partridge & Hare's Ear] across and downstream into the branches. As the fly swept beneath an overhanging limb there was the quick tug and flash of a taking trout and I soon had the pleasure of bringing in a 9" brown trout for release. . . . The next cast drifted so far under the brush pile that I was sure the fly would hang up. Sure enough the line tightened, but when I lifted the rod a very nice trout thrashed upstream. I fought the big brown carefully and eventually slid the extremely fat 13" fish onto the bank. Its girth was unbelievable, maybe equal to 4/5 of its total length, and I was curious about what it had gorged itself on. So I killed this fish, tried the willow bend for another 15 minutes, and went home. The large brown had 4 full-sized adult crayfish in its digestive tract, hence its huge girth. In this it resembled

a 12" trout I caught in June, which was also jam-packed with crayfish. A common pattern on the Onion?

I learned early on that crayfish, even large adult crayfish, are relished by trout in Wisconsin streams. Every season I catch trout, especially browns, whose abdomens are crunchy to the touch because of all the crayfish they've eaten. I also think that I had a better handle on what trout were really eating and why they took my flies in those early years, when I killed many more trout than I do now. I never killed a trout without dissecting their gut and carefully examining what I found there. The evidence about what they'd been eating when I caught them was right there in front of me with no guesswork. Now I release almost all of my trout, but sometimes I get a nagging feeling that I'm only making assumptions about why the fish take my flies. I construct nice, tidy, direct cause-and-effect stories that satisfy my analytical mind, but the stories are probably fiction more often than I'd like to believe.

30 October 1986, Sauk Creek, Ozaukee County. Dry weather again this week as the end of autumn approaches. Sauk Creek was lower this morning, but there were still plenty of fresh-run Chinooks, cohos, and brown trout running. I took several large salmon from the Corner Bend upstream to the Outlet, but the fish of the day was a 28", ten-pound brown from the lower end of the Church Pool on a #8 Green-butt Skunk. I thought about mounting this trout, but released it. It was a fine morning's fishing with my new 9½' salmon rod—Cabela's replaced the one that broke on October 3 while fighting another big Chinook salmon. Cohos seem to be peaking with many fish in the tributaries. Results for today—fourteen coho salmon 24-26", 4-6 pounds; twenty-one Chinook salmon 31-38", 10-18 pounds; two brown trout, 24", 4 pounds and 28", 10 pounds respectively. #4 Purple Heron & #6-#8 Green-butt Skunk, 10 lb. Maxima Chameleon.

From the autumn of 1982 through the summer of 1988 I lived close to several Lake Michigan tributary streams, and I could fish them whenever the water was right and I had the time. In contrast to the large rivers that flow in from the Michigan side of the big lake, Wisconsin's Lake Michigan tribs tend to be small and low-flow except after a rain. To fish many of them successfully at that time, an angler had to live close by or have a friend who could be contacted to see if the water levels were right for good fishing. When the water was high, especially if the stream was falling and clearing after a good rain, Teresa and I had some amazing days and gained lots of experience playing big migratory trout and Pacific salmon on fly rods. In looking over my journals from those years, I find that my most productive day of this kind of fishing was 1 November 1987, when I caught 40 Chinook salmon, 19 coho salmon, and 3 brown trout between 11 a.m. and 3:15 p.m. using traditional steelhead flies like those mentioned above. I quit at 3:15 because my wrists and forearms were worn out. In those years my largest steelhead was a polychrome 30-inch Skamania-strain that weighed 8 pounds (1987) and a 31-inch Chambers Creek–strain that weighed 12 pounds (1984). My largest Lake Michigan brown trout (1983) was 29 inches long and weighed

11 pounds. The Chinooks topped out around 40 inches and 25 pounds. It might surprise you, but I really don't miss this fishing too much. The problems were the setting and the amount of fishing pressure that I sometimes had to deal with on the larger streams that were more suited to fly fishing. I was catching Alaska-type fish, but eastern Wisconsin just wasn't Alaska. Then too, I didn't hunt in those years. Now I look forward to October and November as good months to chase a pointing dog through the woods and fields while carrying a racy 20-gauge double, and deer season in Wisconsin is for deer hunting.

9 June 1989, Castle Rock Creek, Grant County. A weekday; a good day for getting up early and going out to CRC in hopes of getting some of the large trout I saw on my last trip there. I parked on the upper reaches near Castle Rock Spring and Doc Smith Branch about 5 am, rigged up with a shrimp and headed across the meadow. CRC was in great shape; the waters of Doc Smith Branch are no longer throwing in volumes of silt and as a result the creek has reverted to a classic limestone stream bubbling and rippling over beds of elodea and watercress, just as it did twelve years ago when I first fished it! I started at the tail end of a pool where I'd seen big trout back in April. After a few minutes my strike indicator pulled under, but when I struck it was only a baby rainbow. I took several just like it today; perhaps the State has stocked them recently. I kept at it, but no decent trout took. Then at the head of the run, a nondescript looking spot, the indicator quietly sank below the surface and I struck a good fish. The trout rolled and put up the basic

brown trout battle, and as the battle wore on I realized this was a really big fish. We duked it out all the way to the tail of the run before I gently landed, measured, and weighed the fish in the net before releasing it. 21" and 3/4 lbs on a #14 Scud! It was a good morning and the sun wasn't even up yet! . . . Since the day was overcast, Teresa wasn't interested in warmwater fishing and we went back to CRC after lunch. This time I was determined to learn from this morning's mistakes. I rigged a 5x leader to which a #16 Partridge & Hare's Ear was attached (this morning's fish were taking it, probably as an emerger) and approached the bridge pool from the other side. This time the fishing went well and coaxed five good browns from this pool. . . . I tried a few downstream pools and runs below the CTH "Q" bridge. The first pool looked great, but I approached it wrong and put down all the rising trout. The next pool just didn't produce, and I waded through it before climbing out into the screen of bank side grasses. The deep run above looked promising. I cast over the tail of it and immediately took a good 12" brown. The next cast extended farther upstream, the fly drifted back, and suddenly a really big brown slid out from the bank side cover and inhaled it! I struck hard and broke off the fish!! . . . A few more casts up into the run— another big brown (the same one?) slides out and takes the fly; this time I have him! After a hard fight that was chiefly a tug-o-war after the fashion of a big carp, I landed the fish—a huge male brown trout with brilliant red sides & spots that taped out at just over 20"—a great fish. . . . Then at the head of the run another outsize trout had the fly. Several minutes later and about 30 *yards downstream I had the fish—a beautiful 20" rainbow! Unbelievable! The riffle upstream was narrow and shallow, but the water seemed to deepen a bit near the opposite bank and I sent a speculative cast up, let it drift back a bit, then pulled in line preparatory to making another cast farther upstream. As the fly skittered back toward me an unbelievable trout rolled up from the bottom and inhaled it; since I was in the act of casting I hooked it solidly! The huge fish leaped and thrashed downstream with me running after it, trying to keep it out of snags and weeds. When I brought the trout to hand its girth was too large for my hand to grip, so I cradled the big fish in the water—a beautiful rainbow—while gently removing the fly and measuring its length—23"! A marvelous fish on a #16 wet fly. My only regret was that I had left the camera in the car during all this, but the memories of a perfect day on a perfect spring creek will live on with or without pictures. . . . I followed a few shallow braided channels upstream until I was only a bend or two below the Q bridge. . . . A large pool spread below a riffle, and I cast over the tail, dropping the tiny soft-hackled wet fly onto the surface from a safe distance downstream. A large trout inhaled the fly confidently and I set the hook into a kyped male brown that threshed in the tail shallows angrily before streaking upstream. I called to Teresa as I fought the fish, then held a fantastic 21" brown up for pictures before releasing it. My fifth trout of the day of 20" or more!*

That was one fine day even for Castle Rock Creek, which is well known as a good place to catch a lunker trout on a fly. What still surprises me now as I look back on it is that so many big trout were taken on such small flies, a #14 scud and a #16 soft-hackled wet fly. I've had a few other days like this one on Castle Rock and a few other places around the Driftless Area in the years since, but on those occasions I fished big streamer flies. It took me thirteen years of fly fishing to crack the twenty-inch mark for an inland trout, a bright September brownie that rolled out from beneath a submerged branch and inhaled a floating #12 Letort Cricket. During those thirteen years I remember feeling pretty meek and inadequate when I talked to other fly fishers, many of whom seemed to catch twenty-inch trout almost every time out. One instance on Rowan Creek was typical. I met two anglers coming off the stream as I was walking down, and we chatted for a bit. When they found out that I lived nearby and fished the Rowan regularly, one of them said, "Boy, you must get a lot of twenty-inchers, huh?" "Uhhh, no," I replied, "actually the biggest brown I've ever caught here was seventeen-and-a-half inches." "You gotta' be kidding! The creek's full of 'em!" "No, that trout was the biggest." After a few more pleasantries the two anglers sauntered off, but just before they were out of range a thought struck me and I called out to them. "Excuse me, but do you actually measure the big trout you catch?" There was a moment's pause. Then the answer floated downstream. "No. We just know!" With my background in the biological sciences I had naïvely assumed that when somebody told you they'd caught a twenty-inch trout, they'd measured it in centimeters too for the sake of accuracy and precision. But I'm telling you right now, one of the biggest secrets in fly fishing is that very few twenty-inch trout ever go up against the unforgiving reality of a fiberglass tape measure. The best way to catch a lunker of any species is simply to estimate things like length and weight. Peter Grimm is the only angler I know who routinely underestimates the true dimensions of his fish. Pete's a card player too though, and maybe he's smart not to tip his hand.

12 January 1992, Big Green River, Grant Co. Rain settled in this afternoon as it appears we're in for some storms and wet weather for the next few days. Perhaps winter will make a long-awaited return. At any rate Teresa and I figured we'd beat the weather, fish the Big Green this morning, and then head home to watch the NFL Playoffs. Unfortunately we found no available water. Anglers in numbers were working every available stretch of stream by the time we arrived. In fact, cars were evenly spaced all the way down to the CTH "K" bridge a couple of miles below Werley. We tried to fish in a few spots, but it was pretty hopeless.

So there's one way to have a bad day on trout water. Even in the middle of winter back in 1992 we were seeing occasional days of angler saturation on the larger spring creeks, especially on weekends. This tends to happen because of the way fishing works on small Driftless Area trout streams compared to large western rivers like the Yellowstone or the Missouri. Large rivers have lots of fishy territory and can accommodate many wading anglers per mile of stream. If trout are feeding I can fish for hours on a large river and move only only a few hundred yards during that time. But on a small spring creek that has comparatively little internal volume and area, I may cover two or more linear miles in five or six hours of fly fishing. When you have several anglers who don't know each other fishing this way, there can be conflicts on a small spring creek. I admit I'm looking forward to retirement so that I can take my fishing days during the week and do my bit to reduce the army of weekend anglers marching across the Wisconsin countryside. In recent years I've noticed that angler density is increasing on local lakes too. This season (2010), Teresa and I haven't been able to fish parts of nearby Devils Lake because some of the better places are dotted with boats every day of the week. Southern Wisconsin's lakes work hard, even during the winter. I think some species of fish, northern pike for instance, get more fishing pressure during the winter ice-fishing season than they do during the rest of the year.

I may lobby Teresa to retire to a place where there are fewer people per square mile; at any rate, I'm considering it now for the first time in my life. It's hard to say how much the Internet has affected this aspect of fishing. On the one hand a quantity of fishing information that used to be harder to obtain is readily available, but the *quality* of that information? Let's just say I'm getting wrinkles from smiling. I like the Internet for checking on weather, stream flows, et cetera, before I commit to fishing somewhere far from home, and I like to check Trout Unlimited websites so that I know when and where chapter campouts, state council meetings, and the like are being held. In that way a lot of angler congestion can be avoided. I call one other person fishing where I want to fish "angler congestion." It's not that I don't like fishing with people, it's just that I really like fishing alone.

30 April 1995. Marsh Marigolds have appeared in places. Dutchman's Breeches are in bloom on the rocky,

south-facing bluffs. Chironomid hatch is peaking on Devil's Lake. Yellow-rumped Warblers and several other warbler species seem packed together in the thickets on the SW corner of Devil's Lake. Dandelions and Daffodils beginning to overrun civilized areas.

Here's one of the nifty things you can do with a fishing journal: keep track of phenology, or the seasonal timing of natural events. Anglers have long known that fly hatches can be roughly predicted by looking for connections to flowering times for common plants; dame's rocket and the sulphur hatch is just one example. Teresa works for the Aldo Leopold Foundation in Baraboo, and through the foundation we've met the surviving children of Aldo and Estella. Nina Leopold Bradley had phenology notes going back about seventy years, and she told us that events like the first frog choruses and the first pasqueflowers in spring are happening three to four weeks earlier today than they did in the 1940s.

8 May 2004, Devil's Lake, Sauk Co. Overcast with threatening rain; calm (70F) at first, with sudden NW wind squall at 6:45 pm. No insect activity. Thought I'd run over to Devil's Lake this evening, wade the NW corner and spin-fish for bass with twister tails and soft plastics. Wore my Filson Duckbill cap and a rain jacket, and rubber hip boots because I didn't want to putz around with breathables & wading brogues. Waded out as planned and caught one largemouth bass 14". With a strong front approaching it looked like it was going to be an evening with fast action and lots of fish. Then the sun came out from behind a cloud. That's the first thing that went wrong. In the momentarily warm sun I pushed back the hood of my rain jacket and kept casting. Minutes later it clouded over again and I saw what looked like a small model sailboat skating along the surface of the lake next to me. I looked around, but I was the only one there at the moment. Hmmm. Then a squall came up from behind me and I pulled my hood back up. That's when I realized that the model boat sailing boldly out into the Lake with the squall behind it was really my trademark Filson Duckbill Cap, floating along upside down on its waxed cotton fabric with the hollow part up in the air acting as a sail and the duckbill as the rudder. I waded out to get it, but when I reached the waterline with my hip boots the hat was just barely out of reach. No problem, I thought. I'll just cast my twister-tail into the hat and retrieve it that way. No dice. Cast after cast landed on all sides within an inch of the hat, but never quite in it. Filson Duckbill kept floating further and further away during this time. Finally I said to hell with it and waded in to get it. Water was up to my chest; hat was still just out of reach. Said to hell with it again and waded out farther. Water was up to my chin; hat was still just barely out of reach. Damn Lake water is cold in early May! Said to hell with it again and began swimming after hat. Cold water may have had something to do with decision. Can't swim in flooded hip boots like I used to be able to when I was 25. Gave up on hat and started struggling back to shore. Lost Cabela's IM-6 graphite spinning rod and Shimano Spirex reel somewhere about this time. Got back to where I could stand, but too *exhausted to walk out of lake with flooded hip boots. Collapsed to hands and knees and crawled out sputtering. Quite a crowd of people on bank by then, most with cell phones. One guy said he was thinking about calling 911 if I went under. Laid flat on my back with feet in air to empty water out of hip boots. Shocked several ladies. Got up, walked nonchalantly back to truck and went home. Went on the internet and ordered new rod, new reel, and new Filson Duckbill cap. Didn't get blanked though—caught one bass! Fished 6:30 pm–7:00 pm.*

As I said, all of us have some tough days on the water from time to time. But I think this last journal entry illustrates the true value of the Internet for the angler.

Spiders and Flies

Spring officially begins when Teresa and I hitch the long canoe trailer to the truck and drive off into the hill country of southwest Wisconsin in pursuit of sunfish. Bluegills, crappies, rock bass, pumpkinseed sunfish, and sometimes green sunfish are the usual targets on these trips, but we get enough surprises in the form of bass, trout, pike, or even the occasional muskellunge to keep us happy. Neither of us can resist "road birding" as we drive along quiet country roads to the lake, veering first to one side and then the other as we point out favorites like indigo buntings, rose-breasted grosbeaks, and American goldfinches. Neighbors say they can tell it's the Searocks rolling past by the sinuous trail of dust we leave behind as we corkscrew down the gravel byways. Teresa counters that a zigzag path was used successfully by our navy in WWII as a defense against submarines. It still works; we haven't had a single problem with a sub or a torpedo while on a fishing trip.

Upon reaching the lake Teresa takes her customary seat in the bow of the canoe while yours truly is demoted to a secondary role as guide/trolling-motor/fish-unhooker in the stern. Experience has taught me to wear a broad-brimmed Australian bush hat and a tough denim shirt while guiding fly fishers in a canoe. Hardly a day goes by without my getting ticked in the hat by the rubber-legged bluegill spiders that Teresa sends artfully across the still waters. Her targets are the bedding areas which in spring are constantly patrolled by protective panfish and bass; if I get in the way of her back-cast, that's my problem. Of course I wouldn't have it any other way. We both learned to fly fish on panfish and bass, and I still think it's one of the best ways to introduce a beginner to the sport. Many seasons have come and gone since those days, but Teresa and I still get the same kick out of quality bluegill and bass fishing as we did when we were kids.

If bluegills and other sunfish commonly reached the twelve-to-fifteen-inch mark, we might give up trout entirely and spend the rest of our days in happy pursuit of these disc-shaped natives of the still ponds, river backwaters, and slow-moving streams. About the time when lilacs and flowering crabapples reach full bloom in Wisconsin, sunfish hit surface bugs and flies with more gusto than any other freshwater fish. It's common to see a hole in the water a yard long as they take the bug with a distinctive *smack* that sounds like over-amped teenagers on their first kiss. It's a surprise to bring in a fish that's much smaller than the amount of water it displaced when it hit. Bass run bigger but strike much more delicately; often the bug simply disappears as it is sucked below the surface by a hungry bigmouth.

A distinct hierarchy exists among the warm-water game fish and panfish. The pumpkinseed sunfish takes top honors in our well-ordered universe; both of us consider the pumpkinseed to be the golden trout of the sunfish family. Pumpkinseed sunfish are much less common than bluegills in the places we fish, and the vibrant colors of the males during the breeding season must be seen to be appreciated. Male pumpkinseeds in full spawning dress rival even the most colorful denizens of tropical reefs. Bluegills occupy a close second place in the hierarchy. Again the males wear the brightest orange bellies, which is why bluegills are called "sunnies" in the eastern USA. Light blue highlights darken to cobalt blue or green across the back of the male bluegill. Females are olive green above and yellow below. There's nothing quite like the stout resistance of a bull bluegill on the end of a line, the little fish turning in tight circles as it tries to set the full width of its round body perpendicular to the canoe. Bass, both largemouth and smallmouth, occupy the final place on the podium, and we commonly take fish up to three pounds on our homemade bluegill spiders. Crappies, rock bass, and green sunfish round out our catch for a typical day on the lake. On rare occasions we catch pike or muskies that attack our panfish as we're bringing them into the canoe.

As in trout fishing, sunken flies can be deadly, but surface flies and bugs are much more fun to fish. I tie our famous bluegill spiders on long-shanked #10 hooks (TMC-200R). The body is a simple prefab foam body sold by many fly shops and mail-order catalogs; green, black, gray, brown, and yellow are all effective. Precut bulk rubber legs are the only other material in the pattern. I prefer white or yellow legs on a gray body, while Teresa routinely outfishes me using a yellow-bodied bug with black legs. In making the bug, we start by lashing two rubber legs lengthwise along the hook, so that one inch extends forward of the eye (antennae) and two or three inches hang off the end of the hook in back. Then the body is lashed to the hook in two places in an attempt to emphasize the three-segmented body plan of dragonflies, damselflies, wasps, bees, and other tasty, crunchable insects that fish commonly eat. Last to go on are two pairs of transverse rubber legs, one pair tied into each body constriction, the legs extending outward an inch or so to either side. These bugs are light, trim, and easy to cast even with a three-weight line, but the rubber legs sticking out in all directions give an impression of much larger bulk and mass when floating on the water. The bluegill spider has the same silhouette, shadow, and surface impression as a bass bug but much less air resistance. We favor large-sized bodies and relatively large hooks, since they weed out the troublesome silver dollar–sized panfish in favor of big "bulls" in the eight-to-eleven-inch class.

For this season's first panfish outing, Teresa chose a small impoundment folded into the grassy uplands that rise sharply south of the Wisconsin River, toward the crest of Military Ridge. During the late 1950s a tall earthen dam was built across the upper reaches of a small trout stream. It flooded two narrow valleys and formed a handsome lake, well protected by ochre sandstone cliffs and tall white pines that whisper in the breeze. Today we question the wisdom of such a sizable alteration in the landscape, but at that time the change was seen as "progress." Brown trout can still be found in the stream below the dam, and a very cosmopolitan fish population has grown up in the lake above. Surprisingly, and to my mind importantly, there are no carp. Since most of the watershed is within the boundaries of a state park, there is very little agricultural runoff into the lake. In its clear, carp-free water the spring fly fisher can enjoy high quality sport for panfish and bass as they spawn, forage, and protect their nests in plain view of anyone with polarized sunglasses.

On this day a stiff breeze out of the northeast surged down the length of the lake and pushed a lot of warm water into the bays on the western side. Since one of these was right near the boat landing we didn't have to paddle very far to find fish, and my job as guide was an easy one. For four hours we enjoyed rare sport, catching about a hundred fish between the two of us. Eighty percent of these were bluegills, with the rest about equally divided between largemouth bass and pumpkinseed sunfish, and all of them taken on top with our bluegill spiders. The fish of the day was a broad, deep, moss-backed specimen of a pumpkinseed sunfish that Teresa caught. It still ranks as the largest pumpkinseed we've ever seen and was pretty close to the Wisconsin state record at the time. The "pie-plate pumpkinseed" pushed the measuring tape a bit past eleven inches and weighed more than a pound. All the while we fished in water that was so shallow that I simply pushed my paddle deep into the soft muck of the bottom to hold the canoe in position. Many other anglers were on the lake with us, but they couldn't take their deep V-hulled bass boats, festooned with trolling motor(s) and assorted electronic aids, into the skinny water where the fish were.

So we sat together in the calm bay on a sunny May afternoon and fished, telling stories now and then as we recalled other days in other years. There was the time I was paddling my sister Jill and Teresa on this same lake, both women fly casting with the enthusiasm of the newly converted and completely focused on getting their bluegill spiders in front of actively feeding fish. I cinched up the croakie on my sunglasses, pulled the Australian bush hat down over my ears and hunched over in my seat while fly lines whistled past both sides of my head and flies bounced off the brim of my hat. The June sun was warm, and I waited patiently for a lull in the action to exchange my heavy fleece pullover for a T-shirt. Finally there was a pause while Jill and Teresa checked their knots and hooks. Taking advantage of the opportunity, I pulled off the fleece sweatshirt and dug around in my pack for the T-shirt. Precisely at that moment of greatest vulnerability, a nice-sized bass with a wicked sense of humor slashed at a dragonfly some thirty feet out from the canoe. Both women immediately raised their fly rods and tried to shoot thirty feet of line with no false casting. Slack line was whipping everywhere and before I could protest I found myself solidly hooked in both shoulders.

Then there was the young boy fishing from shore with his parents on a long, golden evening in early June. The little guy was quick to notice that Teresa and I were casting differently from everybody else on the lake, and he asked his mom what sort of fishing we were doing. Wise to the ways of anglers, she patiently explained that we were *fly fishing*, that flies were tiny lures traditionally made from fur and feathers to imitate insects that fly near the surface of the water. Since the flies are far too light to be cast with conventional tackle, the fly fisher casts the heavy line back and forth, gradually increasing the distance while the fly just goes along for the ride. When the distance is right, the angler stops casting and allows the fly to fall on the water in a good place. "Oh," said the boy, and there followed a long silence while he pondered this brave new angling method. "But what are they fishing for? Frogs?"

Dame's Rocket

She was waiting for me there, in the shade of a tall oak beside the river. I turned off the highway into the Ellsworth Rod and Gun Club and let the big green truck roll to a stop by a line of whitewashed posts at the brow of the slope leading down to Wisconsin's Rush River. I wasn't surprised to see her. I expected she would be there in the very heart of June, just as I expected the eternal river to be there, and the mayflies, and the trout. But catching her scent as I pulled on wading brogues and strung a long, willowy fly rod evoked a flood of memories, of other rivers and other years long past, and of other late spring days as perfect as this one. I went over to see her as soon as the leader was rigged with a pair of nymphs and I'd donned the trout fisher's uniform of burnt khaki, pale green, and nut brown that helped keep me invisible to the fish. By contrast she was dressed in a crown of vivid lavender petals atop tall green shoots, as befitted one whose name was *Hesperis matronalis* in the ancient tongue, "lady of the evening star" as near as I could make it in English. Dame's rocket is her common name, and the bloom of her presence by the waterside meant that large numbers of yellow mayflies, known as *sulphurs*, would dance over the broad riffles of the Rush at twilight.

The day was fine, the first clear morning after a series of overcast, showery days. Since the sulphurs weren't due until evening, I decided to spend the morning drifting deep nymphs through the big pools, fast runs, and pocket water where the Rush tumbles around the wide turn below the Rod and Gun Club. There was more fast water upstream. This stretch of the Rush was made for nymph fishing.

I cut through the woods so that I could enter the river at the very bottom of the stretch. The shadows beneath the trees were filled with signs that the long Wisconsin spring was finally giving way to high summer. False Solomon's seal, with its dark green oval leaves, was nearly bloomed out. Campion and oxeye daisies showed in patches where shafts of sunlight slipped through the boughs overhead. Cow parsnip towered over the path in places, and I glanced at old scars from parsnip burns on my forearms. Once at a seminar devoted to the problem of weedy, nonnative plants in the Badger State, I remarked to a fellow biologist that I'd been burned by wild parsnip many times over the years. "Slow learner!" she remarked. "No," I replied quietly, "trout fisherman." Send an angler and a nonangler on a walk beside a stretch of wild river and I'll wager that the angler is far better at interpreting and drawing inferences from what he or she has seen. The very act of fishing demands a keen eye for observation of fine details, so much so that anglers can suffer from perceptual blindness. Then we stumble into muskrat holes and get burned by wild parsnip for the dozenth time, to the amazement of our friends and colleagues.

The trees ended suddenly. I pushed through a dense stand of reed canary grass and stood on the edge of one of Wisconsin's finest trout rivers. The Rush has a distinctive fragrance in June, a unique blend of limestone, spring water, wildflowers, and trout. I took a moment to breathe deeply and savor this essence of June. Then I got down to business, unhooked the nymphs from the keeper ring, and began casting.

Upstream nymph fishing to invisible, nonrising trout is very effective, but it is also very demanding. One reason is that the angler must read the water to decide where an invisible trout is holding. A second reason is that nymph fishing is a game played in three spatial dimensions. The angler must cast the flies so that they have time to sink to the trout's depth as well as pass over the place where the trout is likely to be holding. Finally, the upstream nymph fisher is bedeviled by drag to an even greater degree than the dry fly angler, because water at the surface moves faster than water near the bottom of the river where trout usually hold.

I was standing at the edge of a shallow riffle and letting the flies drift through a deep run across from me. Here most of the Rush piled up against the opposite bank before sluicing off downstream. The current was fast and choppy against the bank on the outside edge of the turn, but nearer to me was a slow, deep eddy where the water actually spun around and flowed slowly upstream. Between the fast water racing down and the slow eddy moving up was a seam or current break, a vertical layer of water that separated the two opposing currents. The seam was my target. For flies I had a tandem rig with a #12 Gold-ribbed Hare's Ear Scud at the end of the 4x tippet and a

#16 Sawyer Pheasant Tail Nymph trailing on a fifteen-inch piece of
5x. I cast the nymphs to the top of the seam and a bit to the right so
they would drift downstream along the edge of the current break.

I used a strike indicator pegged in place about four feet above the
lead fly, but even with an indicator many strikes went undetected.
It's rare for the indicator to be pulled under by a trout. Anybody
can see that. Most of the time I strike to small bumps or hops, or to
slight rocking motions of the indicator as it drifts downstream. Less
experienced fly fishers are often mystified as to how I know when to
set the hook. To be honest, much of this has become ingrained and
automatic after so many years of fly fishing. As in any athletic sport,
with long practice and countless repetitions, fundamental skills
become unconscious. We no longer have to think about them. They
simply happen, just as when typing we don't consciously think about
what our fingers are doing; our thoughts simply appear in print as if
by magic.

So I cast the team of nymphs up to the top of the seam, and as
they drifted back I stared at the orange indicator with the single-
minded intensity of an osprey. It took several casts, but finally the
indicator made a little downstream hop and I struck the solid weight
of a good fish. Trout in swift, cool water and fat from feeding in a
productive stream fight like mad, and this particular trout was no
exception. The rod bent in a satisfying arc and vibrated from tip
to butt as the fish bored deep among the rocks in an effort to hide
beneath them, rub out the fly, or cut the leader on a sharp edge.
Failing in this, the trout writhed to the surface and somersaulted over
the river. With a barbless hook, a jumping, head-shaking trout has a

better than even chance of throwing the fly. And so it proved; the little scud came free and the whole business pinballed back over my shoulder into the wicked clutches of a six-foot cow parsnip. Leader, tippet, and flies were tangled in a hopeless mess that took ten or fifteen minutes to extract and sort out. Such is fly fishing.

When I got back in action the nymphs proved their worth by taking a beautifully marked fifteen-inch brown trout from fast, broken water at the top of the run. By the time I reached the big, slow corner-bend below the Rod and Gun Club I'd taken several good browns and many smaller trout. But when I rounded the corner and looked upstream toward the fast runs at the head of the pool, I saw it was time to change tactics.

It was almost noon. The sun was high and bright, a good hatch of tan caddis flies was in progress, and trout were rising in bunches, feeding aggressively. Off came the nymphs and the indicator. On went a couple of feet of 5x tippet and a dark tan #16 CDC Caddis that I'd bought at Lund's Hardware in nearby River Falls.

Rise after rise showed quickly and repeatedly in the run about thirty feet upstream from where I stood. From the quick cadence of the rises I knew the trout would give me instant feedback about my choice of flies. The first cast dropped the fly just in the center of a feeding lane occupied by a good fish. The fly drifted back. Time stood still. Suddenly the trout took it with a popping rise, just as he'd taken the naturals. Business was very brisk for the next hour and a half as I was constantly casting, playing fish, releasing fish, or cleaning off the slime and drying the fly for another go. I took fat, hard-fighting trout with the clockwork regularity that only comes with a good hatch and the right fly. There were no refusals, and every trout took the fly *with the same rise form that was seen when it took the naturals.* This is how to judge whether a trout takes the fly for the natural insect, or out of aggression, competition, or for some other reason.

By one o'clock the caddis hatch had petered out and the morning rise was over. Both the trout and I needed a midday siesta. I drove up to Ellsworth for lunch and spent a quiet afternoon tying flies on a picnic table in a city park. It was cooler beneath the spreading shade of two large maple trees, although the breeze played merry hell with my tying materials.

At four thirty I was back on the Rush, scanning the water from a high vantage point on top of a concrete bridge. Upstream from the bridge a set of riffles extended to the junction with Lost Creek, after which the big river turned away from the road. Below the bridge was a smooth, gravelly flat of shin-deep water where the banks retreated to either side and the river spread out.

Unlike many anglers I was attracted to the thin water on the long flat, perhaps because such "waste water" was common on the eastern rivers I fished as a teenager decades ago. On those hard-fished trout streams, flats were attractive because hardly anybody fished for the selective, easily frightened trout that lived in them.

As I watched intently from my perch on the bridge, one trout after another revealed itself with quiet rises here and there across the wide flat. In one place a fat brook trout sipped something invisible from a bubble line. Several yards away a good-sized brown occupied a choice lie beside a fallen tree, and divided its time between feeding and running off two or three other brown trout that occasionally drifted too close to its place near the log. After twenty minutes of watching from the bridge, I was surprised at the number of trout that were holding and actively feeding in what looked like barren water at first glance.

A deliberate, heron-like approach was called for. I lengthened the leader to sixteen feet and tapered it down to a long 6x tippet. For a fly I picked a #18 CDC Caddis with a dirty yellow body, a simple and versatile pattern that to a trout might suggest any of a half-dozen types of insects. Few Wisconsin trout streams can match the Rush for its density and diversity of invertebrate life.

I made a wide detour downstream of the bridge and slipped into the river below the tail of the flat. Then, sliding my feet along the bottom and wading so slowly that not one ripple of water pushed upstream, I entered the flat and began casting to the nearest trout. It was a fishing chess game.

Every move was carefully considered on its own merit and for its effects on future moves. Trout that were easy to see from the bridge were surprisingly difficult to locate once I was in the water, and again I spent a great deal of time watching the river for rises. Often I saw a rise without a trout. The fish were invisible in the flat light of late afternoon and the rises might have been made by ghosts. Such fishing is absorbing, and I had no sense of time passing as I stalked and cast to each trout in turn. Long, looping casts were curved so that the fly settled down a couple of feet upstream from each trout without the leader falling on the fish's head. There was a long wait as the fly drifted back, ever so slowly, waiting, waiting, a rise so small that it might have been a chub or a dace, a turn of the wrist to set the hook, and then a surge of water and the satisfying feel of a heavy trout dancing on the end of the line.

I spent two happy hours fishing the fifty-yard flat, and it was seven o'clock when I moved upstream of the bridge in anticipation of the sulphur hatch. But the flies were late. I still caught trout here and there from the riffles by searching the current breaks around midstream rocks with a single Pheasant Tail Nymph. By eight o'clock I was well upstream of the junction with Lost Creek. A brief rain shower drifted past, soaking me, and then an intense double rainbow arched across the river, backlit by the setting sun. As suddenly as organ music strikes up in church, clouds of sulphurs began helicoptering over the riffles. Within a few minutes it seemed that every trout in the Rush was eating them with reckless abandon.

The air was filled with small mayflies. Flights of swallows, swifts, flycatchers, and waxwings made no visible impact on their numbers. The river boiled and seethed with trout, and as I knotted a #16 Sulphur Comparadun to the end of the leader I thought I could not miss. But the first trout rose to the fly without being hooked, and then another, and another. Something was wrong. It looked like trout were taking the fly and somehow not getting hooked, but I examined the fly carefully and the hook was straight and sharp. After several more "missed fish" I was sure that the fly wasn't right. Daylight was fading and I was getting frantic as a golden opportunity slipped away. I was shaking so hard that I could barely tie on another #16 Comparadun, but this one had a chartreuse body instead of the usual pumpkin-orange dubbing.

I cast nearly straight across the stream to a rise that just spelled "size." The trout rose to the fly, but this time when I set the hook the long rod bent and a thick brown trout cartwheeled across the river.

From that point on the fishing was easy although I soon ran out of daylight. Still the flies hatched, the trout rose, and I kept fishing, on and on into the darkness. The familiar colors of the day faded. Molten silver dripped from coal-black trout that sagged in the net and writhed in shadow. I think they were brown trout, but a big brookie or two might have been among them. Bats replaced the swallows and swifts. Coyotes sang from the ridges.

At ten o'clock I reeled up for the last time. The smell of dust in the damp night air mixed with the lush scent of a June evening as I crossed several pastures and crunched the gravel roads back to the truck. Lost Creek whispered in the gloom where it splashed through the culvert beneath the country lane. Fireflies flashed above the hedgerows. Bright stars wheeled overhead in the rain-washed sky as I swung along. The welcome outline of the truck loomed up out of the deeper shade beside the road, and I was glad to slide the rod into its case and get out of waders at the end of a long day. Then I sat for a while on the tailgate, picking out familiar constellations in the night sky, enjoying the warm darkness and a cold Rolling Rock. I knew then, as all anglers know, that to have a June day like this was worth any sacrifice.

I was teaching high school science when Halley's Comet returned to our neck of the cosmic woods in 1986. To commemorate the event I traveled around to various elementary schools in our district, teaching lessons about comets and organizing evening sessions where students could get a good look, through a powerful telescope, at this "fuzzy star" moving across the heavens. Students in primary grades ask good questions. One that came up often was "Mr. Searock, what's your favorite planet?" One day I wrote an answer.

My favorite planet is Earth, the water planet. I've never grown tired of it, or bored with it, and many of my happiest days have been spent in its wild places, beside rivers, lakes, oceans, and in the company of organisms who, like me, find themselves caught here in the nets of space-time and evolution. I think that in the future as we begin to explore the galaxy, the one sight that will move us to tears will be our own blue planet, growing larger on our forward view-screen as we journey home.

FISHING FINE AND FAR-OFF

It's All Good

Make a hard right turn as you walk into our house and you'll find yourself on the stairs leading to the basement. At the bottom of the stairs is a rod rack. It has to be there because the stairwell is the only place where we have enough floor-to-ceiling height to accommodate the longer rods, as long as fourteen feet for some of the steelhead and coarse-fishing rods. Anyone who fishes could tell a lot about Teresa and me after a brief glance at our rod rack.

This particular rod rack was a Christmas gift from my youngest sister. Jill is a thoughtful soul who's always looking for the perfect Christmas gift for family members and she hit a home run with this one. The rack is octagonal and it stands about four feet tall. The rods are held vertically in a series of slots distributed evenly around the octagonal base. A sort of weather vane carved in the shape of a jumping fish crowns the top, and large brass hooks, shaped like fish hooks, wrap around each rod and hold it in place. With a little finagling the rack can hold a surprising number of rods, and it bristles like a mad porcupine during the winter when we don't have rods stashed in our vehicles. You might be surprised at the distribution; there are eight fly rods, six spinning rods, one spin-casting outfit, and a heavy casting rod rigged with a spinner-bait for muskies.

There was a time when there were two kinds of people: folks who hunted and fished and spent time in the outdoors, and the poor devils who didn't. Anglers looked at rods and reels as tools of the trade, and found enjoyment and satisfaction in using quality tools that were well made. Experienced anglers chose the right tool for the job at hand, and could employ a diverse skill set of tackle and tactics to suit the water type, the season, and the particular species they were fishing for. Outdoor writers like Gordon MacQuarrie and Ray Bergman referred to fisherfolk as "the angling brethren." They assumed that their readers could drop a tiny dry fly over a persnickety brown trout today and cast a big surface plug for bass or pike tomorrow. They also knew the heart-pounding thrill of ducks dropping into decoys or a big whitetail buck standing square in their sights on a frosty November morning. There was more solidarity among outdoors-people fifty years ago than there is now.

Fishing and hunting are religions in the minds of their devotees, and the outdoor community of the twenty-first century is sharply dividing along denominational lines. In Wisconsin, bitter arguments rage between people who fish for trout with bait and those who cast flies, as if a person couldn't do both. Tournament-style bass fishing has evolved into a world of its own, a world of glitter, money, noise, and fame reminiscent of NASCAR racing. Hunters have split into bow hunters, upland hunters, waterfowl hunters, big game, muzzle-loading, and turkey-hunting factions, and each faction seems willing to jealously guard its interests at the expense of the others. All across the American outdoor landscape increasing specialization seems to be the order of the day, and intolerance among the various user groups is growing. There is even growing animosity between consumptive users—people who take fish, game, and other wild crops to eat—and nonconsumptive users—birders, boaters, back-packers, and the like, again assuming that a person can't possibly be both. There seems to be no spirit of compromise. As one angler told me at one of the annual meetings of the Wisconsin Conservation Congress, "If we compromise, we lose half of what we're fighting for." Yes, and if we don't compromise we could very easily lose all of it. So, in the spirit of outdoorsy ecumenism I offer the following Ten Fishing Commandments for Twenty-First-Century Anglers:

I. Although some fishing is better than others, any fishing is better than no fishing. And when I say that some fishing is better than others, I'm mostly talking about the setting. I suspect that most of us would prefer to fish a tumbling mountain stream instead of a city canal, but I also know darned well that if a canal was the only fishing game in town, we'd all be standing shoulder-to shoulder on its banks, casting our flies, lures, and (heaven forbid) bait with the glassy-eyed zeal of true believers. Think of the anglers fishing the River Seine where it flows through Paris, as depicted by generations of French painters. I've never seen any of them shown with a fish in hand, but they're always fishing.

II. Any fish is a good catch, and all fish are worth fishing for. Trash fish? When you can go to your workshop or your laboratory and make a fish from scratch, I'll let you call it a "trash fish" if you want to. Until then, all fish are miracles of creation and should be treated with the respect and admiration they deserve. Yes, there are invasive, nonnative fish like Asian silver carp that are hard to live with. Are the fish to blame or are we?

III. Assuming that the method is legal, the type of rod, reel, pole, or other tackle used by an angler does *not* constitute grounds for disparaging his or her character. I am reminded of a day on the shores of Trout Lake in Yellowstone National Park when Teresa landed and promptly released a seven-pound rainbow trout some twenty-six inches long. As Teresa lifted the big rainbow from the water, everybody could see the bright yellow #8 weighted Woolly Worm clicked firmly in the trout's toothy upper jaw. When the poor fishless beggar standing next to her said, "Well, I didn't travel three thousand miles to fish with weighted nymphs," Teresa giggled and responded with "That's OK—more for me!"

IV. Thou shalt not criticize the modus operandi of a fellow angler until you have fished with him or her for three full days. The habits of fisherfolk are shaped by their home waters, and the variety of water types found across Wisconsin, let alone North America, defies description. How somebody fishes usually makes perfect sense once you see where they're fishing and what they're fishing for.

V. Arguing about knots is silly. Sometimes as I'm tying on a new tippet with a Blood knot, the person with me will chime in with "You know, a double surgeon's knot is stronger." Then I ask "Can you tie a Blood knot?" The answer is always no.

VI. Litter, and you will burn in Hell for eternity. I also believe that time spent picking up litter is not counted against one's allotted time on Earth.

VII. Take your kids fishing, even if you feel like throwing the little buggers in after a few minutes. Take this one step further and make any necessary sacrifices to supply your kids with quality equipment as they grow into the activity, and take them where they need to go to enjoy decent fishing. Time spent together by the water often connects to other happy times. Catch some frogs, skip stones, buy some ice cream, relax in a lawn chair on the bank and read, or take a nap. Shut off all of your electronic devices, slow down, and feel the soft caress of the breeze on your cheek. Breathe.

VIII. It's probably better to let someone else teach your spouse or significant other to fish, especially if you want them to enjoy it and stick with it. I don't really know why this is so, but it is.

IX. Fight the good fight and help those who are trying to help our lakes, rivers, and coastal waterways. We do not own the land, the water, or the wind; we hold these things in trust for the young people who follow us.

X. Always have a cold beverage waiting for you and a friend at the end of a long, hot day.

Redmire Pool at Dawn

Richard Walker was hunting a giant. He had hunted it all season, and as the sky lightened in the east on this misty September morning it revealed a man's face, gaunt and hollow-eyed, a face whose features were sculpted by exhaustion and obsession. Images unbidden haunted his mind: a sickle-shaped dorsal fin cleaving the still water of Redmire Pool, shiny brass scales resting on black silt in the shallows, scales like armor plates more than three inches across; an impossibly large shadow that floated serenely near a downed willow tree one sultry summer afternoon and then faded away like an evaporating cloud.

For a moment Walker turned his gaze away from water and sky, looked down near his feet, and smiled. It always made him feel better to see his rod suspended by its holder and his line looped through the bite alarm. He'd crafted the rod himself, spending many hours planing long strips of Tonkin cane to exacting tapers and then gluing them together to construct a two-piece rod, ten feet long. The finished rod was beautiful and functional; it was made to fish with, not to hang on the wall as a decoration. Like Henry V's sword or a Spitfire fighter, this was a weapon for working days. Walker christened his rod the Mark IV, and went giant hunting.

He knew that giants are best hunted at night. Most of us have fished at night. A late mayfly hatch may keep us on the stream until midnight or a bit later. Hot summer weather may find us casting in the predawn hours. Richard Walker's night fishing involved getting to Redmire before sunset and fishing all night until 9 or 10 a.m. the following day. Imagine putting in a full workweek, then fishing all night Friday and again on Saturday, and still getting up and off to work on Monday morning, with family obligations thrown in somewhere, doing this week after week and ultimately month after month. No wonder Walker looked a bit haggard by September.

Nevertheless, on the night of September 12, 1952, Walker and his usual fishing companion Peter Thomas cast their baits into the water at Redmire Pool, put the Mark IVs in the rod holders, set the bite alarms, and settled down to wait out another long night. It was cold in the darkness. Just after 2 a.m. the sky clouded over, threatening rain. Walker said later that he never remembered being out on a blacker night. The wind died down, and off in the shadows Redmire Pool was becalmed and absolutely quiet. Walker and Thomas dozed. Around 4:45 a.m. one of the bite alarms went off.

Thomas got to the rods first and, turning to Walker, said simply, "It's yours." Walker put the back of his right hand against the line where it spooled off the reel. The hairs on his hand prickled as the line passed over them. Something had taken the bait and was moving steadily away, out into the deep end of Redmire Pool. Slowly, with a deftness borne of long experience, Walker lifted the Mark IV from its holder. The bail of the spinning reel clicked solidly as it engaged. He stood motionless in the dark, rod in hand, waiting, waiting until the line was almost tight. Then he struck with all his strength, a wide, sweeping stroke that ended with the rod up high above his head. The progressive action of the Mark IV hooked the fish without breaking the line, and battle was joined.

Walker said that hooking the fish was like hooking a sandbag. For a sandbag it fought pretty well. The turning point came when the lunker decided to try to hide in a weed-choked tangle of chestnut roots near the dam. Somehow the fish had to be stopped. Walker described the action in his classic *Still-Water Angling*: "I increased pressure. At first it had no effect; then as I bent the rod more, the efforts of the fish became intensified. I knew only a few yards separated it from disaster, and hung on grimly. The rod bent as never before—I could feel the curve under the corks in my hand; but everything held for the two or three minutes that the fish continued to fight his way towards his refuge. Then, suddenly, he gave it up."

The fight continued, but the outcome seemed no longer in doubt. Then, just as Peter Thomas was about to net the huge fish, it ran straight into a submerged clump of brambles. Undeterred, Thomas reached into the brambles, put his hand around the fish's head, turned it around, and guided it back out through the tunnel of thorns into the waiting net. There was just one more problem: Thomas couldn't lift the fish out of the water. Walker set down his rod and waded out to help his friend. He grabbed one side of the net frame, and together the two men hauled the fish out and struggled fifty yards away from the lake over ground mined with tussocks. Then they put down the net and started breathing again. The fish was a giant common carp, *Cyprinus carpio*, the largest they had ever seen, and the largest anyone had ever caught with a rod in England at that time.

All summer Richard Walker had thought about what he would do if he caught a record fish. Now that he'd done it, he simply couldn't kill it. The two anglers kept the carp alive in a keep-sack until they could make a telephone call to the director of the aquarium at the London Zoo. Walker and Thomas were able to weigh the carp on a certified scale before gently carrying the fish to a display tank. Forty-four pounds exactly, and a very popular fish while it lived out the rest of its days on public display in Regent's Park.

Still-Water Angling was published by MacGibbon & Kee the following year and has become a classic. Richard Walker became a truly legendary angler throughout the United Kingdom and Europe, and remains so today long after his death. His Mark IV rod has become an icon among anglers who specialize in fishing for cyprinids like carp, barbel, tench, and bronze bream. Everybody on that side of the Atlantic wants to buy one or build one, just as every pilot dreams of flying a Spitfire.

Not in the United States, however. Most anglers I talk to are unaware of how popular carp are across the Atlantic, and incredulous that a fisherman like Richard Walker could be lionized for catching a carp, no matter how big the "danged scale-fish" was. "What? A trash fish?? I shoot 'em with my bow!" is a common response. How anglers relate to fish like carp provides deep insight into the complicated love-hate relationship that we have with species that are invasive and nonnative where we live.

Teresa and I are no different from anybody else in this respect. Our home in the Baraboo Hills of Wisconsin displays the whole thing in microcosm. Our property is perched on top of a divide between the Wisconsin River and Baraboo River watersheds. On either side of the ridge are two very different aquatic and riparian worlds.

Prentice Creek begins just west of our land and falls east through the narrow defile of Durwards Glen, eventually losing itself in the Wisconsin River. Prentice Creek is two or three feet wide in most places and is barely fishable at all, but it holds a tenuous population of wild, native brook trout, a true ice-age relict population of *Salvelinus fontinalis*. These fish are tiny, incredibly precious, 100 percent native brook trout that few people know about. Prentice Creek also hosts small but persistent populations of native ruffed grouse and American woodcock that live and breed on its banks in company with a suite of native plants.

To the north, Rowley Creek picks up all the seepages and springs of a much larger valley and flows west into the Baraboo River. Rowley Creek originally wasn't a trout stream at all. Sometime during the 1930s a company prospecting for iron ore drilled a system of boreholes along the spine of the Baraboo Hills south of the creek. No iron was found but groundwater flooded the boreholes, which became artesian wells. The influx of clear, cold spring water was so great that it altered the thermal regimen of Rowley Creek to the point where the stream could support trout. Within several years the State of Wisconsin began stocking domestic, hatchery strains of brook trout and non-native brown trout in Rowley Creek, and the rest is history. These domestic-strain trout reproduce naturally and very successfully today, and I see people fishing on Rowley Creek about four days a week during the trout season. Nonnative watercress is common in Rowley Creek and doesn't seem out of place in a riparian plant community that is mostly European. The native sharptailed grouse that were plentiful in the Baraboo River valley as recently as the 1920s have been replaced by nonnative Asian ring-necked pheasants.

Even innocent people are a delicious irony when viewed through this lens. The most invasive, nonnative, habitat-altering, weed-spreading species in Wisconsin is people like me, nonnatives who have come to Wisconsin over the past two centuries. Teresa has a Native American woman on her recent family tree, but I guess I'm a Polarian: a hodgepodge of genes from fishing Poles and fishing Hungarians mix-mastered together and born in the USA with a little silver fishing rod in my hand. I'm the enemy, and there are more and more like me every year. But take my advice and don't ever bring up the issue of human overpopulation in a room full of conservationists. Heck, don't bring it up at all, anywhere; as one writer put it, "We need to make sure that elephants standing in rooms don't become endangered."

People have strong biases in favor of some fish and some methods of fishing, and I've always been curious about why that is. I think it comes down to four factors: the intrinsic qualities of the fish (including whether they're native or introduced), the aesthetic qualities of the fishing method, the setting where fishing takes place, and the socioeconomic class of the angler.

The first "big" fish I ever caught was a carp from Pennsylvania's Delaware River. It weighed just 3½ pounds, but I was six years old and it was far and away the biggest fish I'd ever seen. At that age I didn't know there were "trash" fish, and it never entered my head that such a big, beautiful, hard-fighting fish had no value in the eyes of anyone present except me. Because it was my first big fish, because I caught it at a very impressionable age, and because I caught it from a beautiful pool near the towering cliffs of the Delaware Water Gap in the presence of witnesses including my father, grandfather, and several uncles, carp have always occupied a special place in my heart.

Judged strictly by appearance, a big carp with its bronze scales and red fins is a truly beautiful fish. Compared with a salmon or a trout, somebody asks? Yes; a big, healthy carp is far more beautiful than a dark, rotting Pacific salmon finning weakly in the lukewarm water of the Milwaukee River or a Lake Michigan brown trout covered in fungus. But the carp is an invasive, nonnative species, and today my default position is that I'm opposed to moving any species of plant or animal to places where that species isn't, or wasn't, naturally occurring in recent geologic time. This is a complicated, inconsistent, and hypocritical position for me though. I can condemn the carp, but I can't bring myself to condemn the ring-necked pheasant or the brown trout.

Fly fishing is a very active way to fish, and many people find the graceful dance of fly casting to be more satisfying than any other fishing method. Fly fishing is also great fun for people who like to walk. Personally I much prefer to use the fly rod in situations where the fish that I'm after are concentrated in a relatively small area, in shallow water, and in water that's clear enough to see the fish take the fly. But for covering a large area of water for fish that are spread out, I'll use a spinning or casting rod every time. Part of the decision depends on how the rotator cuff in my right shoulder is feeling on a given day. My body's kind of like an old car with high mileage, and I have to pick and choose my fishing times, places, and methods so that I'm having fun. For me, fishing in pain is not fun.

I think that the quality of the setting where fishing takes place is the single most important factor that determines fishing enjoyment. This is where carp start to lose serious ground among American anglers. Species like trout and grayling are not only beautiful to look at; they are uncompromising about where they live. Brook trout are like canaries in old-time coal mines. Their presence indicates that the stream's water quality is excellent. Cutthroat trout are the Lewis and Clark fish, living symbols of the last unspoiled wilderness areas in the American West. By contrast, carp are often the last fish to die off in polluted, degraded bodies of water surrounded by human development. But where carp are the only fish left, or where carp live at peace with other fish in clear, unpolluted water, they are fun to catch and fun to fish for.

This brings us at last to the dark side of fishing; the effect of socioeconomic class on how we view the activity. Class structure is much more apparent, and openly acknowledged, in the United Kingdom than it is in the United States, but how we view our world, including fishing, has a lot to do with socioeconomic class no matter where we live. One of the reasons I still enjoy carp fishing today is that by engaging in it I'm defying and rebelling against some biases I was taught when I was a kid. It's fun being a rebel and striking a blow for social equality in my own small way. And if by fishing for carp I honor the memory of a truly great angler like the late Richard Walker, then I am proud to do so.

The Choice

A freestone stream was the first trout water that sang to me, and the music of clear, cold water rushing around mossy boulders and tumbling over ledge rock has haunted my thoughts ever since. Bieber Creek caromed down a narrow fold in the misty blue ridges of Pennsylvania, where my aunt and uncle owned the Empathy Gardens resort. Empathy Gardens made its name as a group of secluded cabins in the cool, forested uplands of Berks County. Most of its guests were people from Philadelphia who were trying to escape the heat of the city during their summer vacations. Sometimes my family would stop at Empathy Gardens during trips to visit relatives "back east." On just such a day when I was five years old, my dad lifted me up so that I could see over the parapet of a fieldstone bridge and down into the dark, slightly tea-colored water swirling below. At first I saw nothing but wet rocks, noisy, foaming water, and long lines of bubbles. But with Dad's patient help I finally made out the narrow, wavering shadows of fish holding just in front of the largest rock like dolphins running ahead of a cruise ship, except in this case the water was moving and the "ship" was stationary. We watched the trout for some time as they shimmied back and forth in the current, darting about in search of food and maintaining a pecking order that kept the largest fish in the best position. Little did I realize the powerful spell that those trout cast upon me on that long ago July afternoon. Or perhaps it was the raw force of the loud, rushing water or the sense of mystery in the deep-shaded forest of yellow birch and hemlock that surrounded it, or maybe all these things burned such a deep impression in my young mind that even now, after more than four decades, the experience is as clear in my memory as if it happened this morning. I can still hear the roar of the cascades, and I can smell the drift of pine needles beneath the trees and the musty dampness of the stones along the bank even as I write. Sometimes I wonder if Dad understood the risk of introducing me to those things.

Many years passed before I learned to fly fish, but the fishing passion never died even though we lived in the suburbs of Chicago and my fishing opportunities were limited to a couple of small, sadly degraded ponds and lakes that were within biking distance of our home. I settled for carp, goldfish, bullheads, and a few largemouth bass and panfish because they were the only game in town. A cane pole was the first fishing outfit that I bought with my own money, but sometimes I'd borrow one of Dad's spinning outfits even though he wasn't very pleased about it. All of my fishing at this time was done with live bait: earthworms large and small, and sometimes grasshoppers later in the summer.

I've heard Ohio described as "the sportsman's hell," but looking back I can't think of a bleaker, more depressing place for a young outdoorsman to live than the hundreds of square miles of tract housing that sprang up like mushrooms around Chicago during the late 1960s and early '70s. Nature was hard to find, and what little there was required a car to get to. My fishing options were ugly and very limited, but in an odd way I was better for this. The public library was within biking distance, and I was excited to find a large selection of fishing books in what will always be my favorite Dewey decimal: 799.1. It didn't take me long to discover that most of the books were about fly fishing for trout. I had never seen anyone fly fishing except for Lee Wulff, Curt Gowdy, and Bing Crosby on the *American Sportsman* television show. Even so, when I read Ray Bergman's *Trout* and Robert Traver's *Anatomy of a Fisherman*, I was hooked. I still think that two hallmarks of an accomplished outdoor life are catching a sixteen-inch trout on a dry fly and shooting a ruffed grouse on the wing with a 20-gauge double.

By the time I was fourteen I'd scraped together a fly-fishing outfit. A minimalist by circumstance (odd jobs, paper route money, girls, and an abiding love of the outdoors never yet made a rich man), I had an eight-foot Garcia "Conolon 3-star" green fiberglass fly rod, a Heddon single-action fly reel that was such a bald-faced copy of a Hardy LRH that the parts were interchangeable, a level Cortland 333 #6 floating line, and a Perrine aluminum fly box stuffed with hand-me-down flies (some mounted on snelled loops) from Granddad and various uncles. My folks noticed that a few small items mysteriously vanished from our house, including Mom's nail clippers and Dad's needle-nose pliers. For a leader I just pirated a few yards of Trilene from Dad's spinning reels. With a six-foot piece of 10-pound test knotted to a two-foot strand of 6-pound test "tippet," I was all set. In my first year of fly fishing I didn't have a vest, and I didn't need one. All the tackle I owned fit neatly inside a rubberized canvas creel that did double duty as a fish carrier. I did everything I could to be ready to fish a trout stream with my fly rod if an opportunity came my way.

I had already caught a few trout by this time. One evening at a KOA campground just off of I-70 west of Denver, I fished a tumbling little stream that coursed right next to our campsite and caught a ten-inch rainbow trout. It was exciting to catch a trout from a stream, on my own, even though I caught it on a crappie jig that I fished with a spinning rod. When I was in the seventh and eighth grades, the Village of Schaumburg stocked one of the municipal swimming pools with rainbows in late October and charged people a dollar to catch two fish. Sometimes I tell people that I caught some of my first trout from Illinois's famous Meinecke Pool, which is really true. Crappie jigs were fairly successful between the lane lines in the three- to six-foot-deep areas, but my ace in the hole was Velveeta "cheese" molded onto a hook and fished with a slip-sinker rig in the deep end beneath the diving boards.

Young people everywhere are idealists, and what I clung to was an ideal. We lived in concrete canyons and acres of pavement, first in the city of Chicago and later in the suburbs. I attended a junior high school that had chains and padlocks on most of the exterior doors and a principal who was later prosecuted for "misappropriation of funds." Richard Nixon was president. The Vietnam nightmare dragged on. But in my mind I lived in trout country. Week after week I kept checking the same books out of the library: Ray Bergman's *Trout*, Robert Traver's *Anatomy of a Fisherman*, Ernest Schwiebert's *Nymphs*, Larry Koller's *The Treasury of Angling*, and Howard T. Walden's *Familiar Freshwater Fishes of America*. I set a national record for daydreaming by a ninth grader and I wasn't thinking about sex, well, not always. In my mind I fished the Catskills with Ray Bergman or smoked Italian cigars with Traver beside a remote Michigan beaver pond. I picked dead mayflies from streamside cobwebs in search of clues to match the hatch. I slept in sunny green meadows along some lyrical New England brook, reveling in what Howard T. Walden characterized as "rural peace, unmachined enterprise, and nature left to herself." The spring season was especially bad. I remember walking home from school on the first balmy March afternoons, watching rivers of snowmelt in the gutters and storm drains, and thinking "for today, and maybe all this week, trout could live there . . ."

When school finally let out for the summer we took our annual vacation to southeast Pennsylvania, to trout country. Not great trout country, but there were trout living in trout streams as compared with Cook County, Illinois, where there were almost no trout and certainly no trout streams. The Bushkill in Northampton County was well known among Pennsylvania anglers as a sorry, ugly cuss of a trout stream. Some people called it a working-class trout stream. The river was trapped between gray concrete barriers where it ran through the city of Easton. Believe it or not, there was a catch-and-release area there at one time. Above town the Bushkill's upper reaches were surrounded by tract housing and channelized in the name of "flood control." Pale, flabby hatchery brown trout, rainbows, and palominos were stocked by the Commonwealth three times each season, and most locals quit fishing the stream a week or two after that last stocking day. Still, the Bushkill had a couple of things going for it. Granddad and most of my uncles fished it regularly, and I could pedal my bike there any day I wanted to fish. And pedal I did, three or four days a week, all summer long; wading wet in sneakers and blue jeans, getting soaking wet if it rained and sunburned if it didn't. I don't think skin cancer had been invented yet. Slogging up and down the stream, day after day, and living on a steady diet of peanut butter and jelly sandwiches and Coca-Cola made me leaner, fitter, and browner than I've ever been since. But no trout found their way into my rubberized creel. Sadly, I did hook a few trout that escaped after short fights. It still hurts even today when I think of them. Stream temperatures must have been pretty high, because the fish I did catch were bluegills or *fallfish*, a red-finned minnow native to many eastern trout streams that can run as large as eighteen inches.

All too soon it was August and nearly time to head back home to Illinois. One day my mom decided to make the drive south and west to Berks County, to what she called Pennsylvania Dutch Country then and we call Amish Country in Wisconsin today. Empathy Gardens was on the itinerary, and when Mom mentioned the name something stirred in my head. Dim memories of a breezy midsummer day long before . . . sun-dappled leaves . . . wind in the hemlocks . . .

crashing whitewater so loud that no one could hear me, or they pretended not to . . . Dad holding me up so I could see over the bridge . . . *wavering shadows deep in the water, just ahead of the big rock*. I threw my gear into the trunk of the big AMC Matador and didn't say much during the trip.

My uncle couldn't give me a very hopeful report of the trout fishing prospects when I tactfully brought up the subject at least thirty seconds into our conversation. Years before, when he'd quit a successful civil engineering career to retire to the resort, there had been some fine speckled trout in the stream. He even had pictures of two-pound brookies caught from "the pond," a reservoir behind a small dam that generated electricity for the cabins. However, in recent years the pond had mostly silted in because of runoff from construction sites upstream, and my uncle was in the midst of a long, expensive, and ultimately unsuccessful legal battle to force the builders to leave a buffer strip near the creek and dredge the silt from his pond. "Fish the creek if you want to," he said, "but you're probably wasting your time."

I wasn't discouraged. Bieber Creek couldn't possibly be worse than the Bushkill. I had seen trout in Bieber Creek. I knew they were there. Until that day I had *hoped* to catch a trout on a fly, but now for the very first time I *expected* to catch a trout on a fly. That is the essential difference between the novice fly fisher and the veteran.

The whole day seems like a dream now as I look back down the tunnel of the years. I was shaking so hard I could barely get my fly rod together and the line strung through all the guides. How many times, even today, do I miss that one snake guide in my excitement to get to the river? The fly was a #12 Hare Fly, a scraggly local pattern something like a Gold-ribbed Hare's Ear Nymph that got its finger stuck in an electrical outlet. The dubbed fur stuck out so far in all directions that the overall silhouette of the fly was more like a Bivisible or Woolly Worm. I liked the Hare Fly because I could fish it dry, wet, upstream, downstream, dead-drift, or twitched on the retrieve; the fly could do whatever the circumstances demanded. I still carry a few in my boxes, and every so often I fish one for old time's sake. It's funny how many educated trout that should know better still love this furry little beast of a fly.

As I walked down the gravel lane, cool and shady beneath the spreading branches of yellow birch and hemlock, I was surrounded by the noise of cold, clean water rushing wild and free down the narrow valley. I stepped through a portal. My everyday world no longer existed; it had no power over me, and I was alone and free to do as I wished. There was the fieldstone bridge over the tumbling stream, and as I approached it I slowed to a stop as I became aware that the first significant choice of my life was before me, that it was important and irrevocable. The rest of my time on earth would depend on what I did right now. I could stop deluding myself, turn around, and face reality. I could throw my crude, cheap excuses for tackle back into the car and rejoin the people who said I was crazy to pass up a picnic lunch to go fishing in a stream that didn't have any fish. Or I could cross the bridge.

I crouched down and tiptoed across, staying dead center and not daring to look over the parapet. Then I slipped down to the waterside on hands and knees, making no more disturbance than a dandelion seed in the wind. My first cast was a good one. The fly drifted down the bubble line toward the face of the big rock. There was a flash of boiling gold; the line throbbed, the rod bucked, and a wild trout leaped. There are precious few moments in this life when our ideals are realized, no matter how hard we work to achieve such things, but that was such a moment. Just a foot-long brown trout, a commonplace, but more important to me than all the money, power, or fame in the world. Nature was truly generous that afternoon. More trout were caught, and still more, from plunge pools below stair-step waterfalls and from swirling pockets around boulders polished smooth by the racing water. At the end of the day I laid out my catch on a bed of clean moss. There were four brown trout and one rainbow, from eight to thirteen inches in length. I carefully arranged them from largest to smallest, replayed the details of their capture, and admired their clean lines and carmine spots against flanks of burnished gold. I sat alone in the shadows beside the roaring stream and stared at the trout for a long time. I have never regretted my choice.

Trout Lake

The dry chill of a cold Yellowstone morning greets me as I step outside the tent and start our morning ritual. A thick layer of frost coats the purple fireweed beside the tent. Off to the east rise the sun-splashed heights of Abiathar Peak and the Thunderer, two mountains in the Absaroka Range, which forms the east wall of the Yellowstone Plateau. Behind the picnic table Mount Hornaday is golden in the clear morning light. Just twenty yards from the tent Pebble Creek busies itself cutting and polishing the smooth stones of its wide bed, murmuring the ancient spell of running water as it courses through the campground on its way to Soda Butte Creek, and eventually to the moody Lamar River. The sharp-sour odor of sulfide, blue spruce, and fir is heavy in the air as I clatter about in the truck and pull together the ingredients of a camp breakfast. Soon the little single-burner stove is roaring like a rocket engine, and the strong aroma of fresh, hot coffee is enough to lure even Teresa, a Florida native, out of the warm comfort of her sleeping bag.

Over Pop-Tarts and trail mix we plan and map out the campaign for the day. The upper Pebble Creek meadows are a stiff five-mile hike up the trail from the campground. There jewel-like cutthroats would smash our floating crickets and 'hoppers in every pool and pocket, but neither of us feels up to the steep climb of several thousand feet this morning. Soda Butte Creek and the Lamar are good starters, but heavy rains the past two days have both rivers bank-full and running chocolate with volcanic mud and clay. In the end we decide to spend the morning fishing Trout Lake, one of our favorite places in Yellowstone.

Trout Lake is one of the rarest water types in the park. The rock cradling its twelve-acre surface is mostly dolomite, which exposes the groundwater percolating through it to high concentrations of magnesium bicarbonate. As a result, Trout Lake has a strongly alkaline pH, and its turquoise shallows are unusually rich in trout food for a high alpine lake. Except for Mount Hornaday towering over it, at first glance Trout Lake looks like a giant Wisconsin spring pond. The likeness is more than skin deep. Their aquatic invertebrates are similar, and since Trout Lake is close to a major road and has large, obvious trout patrolling the shallows in plain view, it's quite a popular fishing spot. However, as many anglers have discovered to their chagrin, the big, beautiful rainbow and cutthroat trout can be evil, wicked devils to catch.

Midmorning finds two intrepid Wisconsinites huffing and puffing their way up the trail from the little parking area to the lake. Though it's only a half-mile walk, that half-mile is nearly straight up the side of a steep, boulder-studded moraine. Midwestern lungs lose something at an altitude of eight thousand feet, but we stagger on gamely with our fly rods in hand. Near the top of the moraine is a huge Douglas fir, one of the largest trees in the park, and a convenient rest stop where we can renew our commitment to regular physical exercise. The Douglas fir is an old friend, and we take time to greet it and ask how things have been going in the years since our last visit to Yellowstone.

Over the top of the moraine we go, and then as we clump down a switchback the shores of Trout Lake come into view between the trunks of lodgepole pines. It is absolutely calm, and the blue-green depths gleam like a twelve-acre sapphire in the morning sunshine. We are the first people here today, and we take some skinny-dipping natives by surprise. The family of river otters is unfazed by our presence. They swim toward us clicking, grunting, and snaking nose-to-tail across the lake to the inlet stream, looking for all the world like a many-humped Loch Ness monster. A flock of Barrow's goldeneye ducks, a rare sight in Wisconsin but common in Yellowstone, splash and paddle around near the center of the glassy-smooth expanse of water.

With a wave and a "good luck," Teresa and I separate and begin stalking around Trout Lake in opposite directions. We go slowly, with lots of pauses to scan the water for trout. We soon find out that the unusually hot summer has heated the water to the point where very few trout are cruising the shallows in search of scuds, midges, *Callibaetis*, and damselflies. In a typical year it might take us several hours to work our way around Trout Lake, with many stops to stalk, cast, and tussle with the big cutthroat and rainbow trout that live and breed in its azure depths. This year we do it in forty-five minutes, and when we meet on the far side of the lake near the inlet stream, neither of us has even a tale of a trout to show for our efforts.

After our rendezvous Teresa continues on to a little point of black basalt that juts a few yards out into the lake from the north shore. It's a strategic place to wait for fish. The elevated platform gives her an excellent view over a wide, weedy flat illuminated by sunlight coming in from behind. I walk back to the little bay where the inlet stream pours in and scan the water patiently, forcing myself to concentrate on the task of *seeing* instead of looking. I breathe deeply and bore holes in the water with my eyes. Twenty/fifteen corrected vision is a blessing, but I still have to make an effort to see what is actually in front of me. If I relax, my brain simply takes the easier way and clones in a monotony of submerged weeds and woody debris.

For a long time nothing stirs, but suddenly I'm aware of two large rainbow trout swimming slowly along the edge of a weed bed in about six feet of water. Every now and then one of the fish tips down and roots around in the weeds on the bottom, and judging by the way both fish whirl around and snap their jaws from time to time, the trout are feeding on scuds (*Gammarus*). As I watch, the rainbows glide slowly off to my left and disappear into deeper water that is shot through with sunbeams. Ten minutes later they reappear off to my right. Like many still-water trout, the rainbows are following an elliptical orbit that will take them within casting range every ten to fifteen minutes.

My hands are shaking so much that I struggle to tie a #12 Olive Scud to the 4x tippet. In a few minutes the trout appear on their next pass. I cast the fly well ahead of the fish, allowing enough time for the fly to sink to the bottom when the trout are still fifteen feet away from it. No dice; the rainbows don't show a flicker of interest even when I twitch the scud off the bottom as they pass by. I try again the next time they come gliding around the circuit, but again the trout pay no attention to the fly at all. After they swim off I strip in line to change the fly.

My next trick is a #16 Pheasant Tail Nymph on a long 5x tippet. This time the trout are interested, and for a heart-pounding moment I think that the lead fish is going to inhale the little PTN. But the trout stops, takes a hard look, rejects the fly at the last minute, and turns away. Subsequent tries with the PTN generate no response at all from either trout. An hour goes by and the sun climbs higher above the mountains. I try a few other flies without success. Soon the rising midday breeze will ripple the surface of Trout Lake and sight-fishing will be over for today. Conscious of my limited time, I add a 6x tippet that extends the leader to eighteen feet and tie a #20 Brassie to the sharp end.

This time I cast the fly when the fish are nowhere in sight. I pick a place where I think the two rainbows will swim past if and when they show up on their next orbit. I let the little brassie sink to the bottom. I can't see the fly, but I concentrate on the square meter of bottom where I think it is. Long minutes pass. My back is sore, the surface of Trout Lake is a giant mirror, and my head aches from peering through the glare of the morning sun reflected in it. I'm tired. It's hard to wait until the trout return. Will they return? Am I wasting my time? Then the thick, green-backed rainbows appear magically out of the sunbeams, swimming along in a slow, stately fashion befitting their royal proportions. When they're within a yard of the fly I give the line one good strip. The lead trout suddenly changes direction, swims another couple of feet, and stops. Time stops too, but my heart is pounding hard in my chest. A little flash of white blinks in the depths. I strike, and the big rainbow writhes up to the surface, gills flared in anger, pain, fright, surprise, or maybe all of those things. Then with a sharp, muscular contraction that begins at its head and wrenches its body all the way to its tail the big trout bolts for deeper water. I feel rather than see what happens next: a thump on the rod, which can only have been the trout crashing through a tangle of weeds, then a second, then a third time, and suddenly the line stops moving. I reel in most of a soggy fly line encumbered with weeds and algae. The 6x tippet has sheared off from the drag of all that weight.

I'm boiling with adrenaline. My whole body shakes so hard that it takes an age to rebuild the leader and tie on another brassie. When it's finally done I look out over Trout Lake again. The sunlight sparkles on the surface in a million diamonds, and from her rocky perch Teresa signals me with a friendly wave. I don't really expect another chance at a fish like that, but when I look again there is the second trout cruising along its patrol route as if the first episode had never happened. The rainbow turns and tails away to the more remote part of its beat. Once more I cast the fly and let it sink to the bottom.

In the minutes that follow I rehearse a new game plan in my mind. Minutes later the trout reappears. Again I twitch the fly when the fish is close, and suddenly I'm connected to the trout of a lifetime, a giant green fish with a crimson stripe that must be three or four inches wide. For a few seconds after the strike I have the big trout off balance. This time I keep the line tight, applying maximum side pressure with the rod and refusing to let the trout right itself and recover its bearings. It works. I keep the pressure on and the fish's head off line, slowly walking it farther along the bank and away from the weed beds near the inlet. But just when I think I might be able to win this one, the trout wrenches its head down angrily and bolts off at near light-speed. Beads of water shoot off the line as it hisses through guides. The reel handle spins so fast it's a blur of shiny silver. The Peerless is screeching higher and louder than I've ever heard a fly reel shriek in fresh water. I close my eyes and wince, because I know what is going to happen.

This time it takes only one clump of weeds and the trout is gone, and I am gone, and a sinking feeling hits my chest like a hammer. My knees are weak and wobbly as I reel up and stagger out of the shallows into the sagebrush on the bank. Far out in the lake a giant rainbow trout leaps several times. I can't be sure from this distance, but I think it's trying to shake a #20 brassie and a hunk of 6x tippet from the corner of its jaw. Teresa walks over, exclaiming "Wow! Did you see that fish jumping? It must have gone ten pounds!" "Yes," I answer, softly and absently, "I saw it." Then I find a grassy spot and daydream for a while beneath that wide Wyoming sky, watching clouds built like haystacks, forming and evaporating, rank upon rank marching across the blue vault of heaven from west to east.

That night around the campfire we visit with our neighbor, a professor of English literature from Idaho State University. Every summer he camps at Pebble Creek for a few weeks, reveling in the peace of camp life and catching up on his reading. He's also a veteran fly fisher. The professor's home river is Idaho's tumbling Lochsa, and its fat German brown trout are his teachers and confessors. As sparks crackle in the starlit night I tell the story of the two trophy rainbows, and in a gentle, indirect way he helps me to put things in perspective. We talk about the wolf pups at play on the wide sagebrush flats of the Lamar valley. We talk about bears, about the ever-changing waters of Yellowstone, and about the ephemeral nature of the things that we love. Finally he says, "You know, in a place like Yellowstone, fly fishing for trout is merely a bonus." I know he was right, but even now those two big rainbows sometimes swim into my thoughts, huge and stately as they cruise the emerald deeps of Trout Lake, only to vanish in the sunbeams of my mind.

Devon and Cornwall

In the summer of 2004 Teresa and I flew to England, rented a car, and spent a month poking around the United Kingdom from Land's End north to Cape Wrath. As a fishing excursion this needs a bit of explanation if not outright defense. We could have taken a trip to New Zealand, Chile, Argentina, Alaska, Labrador, or even Mongolia, all of which measure up to the twenty-first-century ideal of the angler's Eldorado. What led us to choose, in the words of the Bard, "This blessed plot, this earth, this realm, this England"? We chose England for the same reasons that a wild brook trout ten inches long has a higher value than a ten-pound carp in the minds of many anglers, the same reasons people will gladly take extreme risks trekking the Rockies in search of rare cutthroat and golden trout. In fishing as in life, the quality and richness of the experience are worth a great deal more than the quantitative outcome in inches or pounds. Our trip was a fly-fishing pilgrimage in the truest sense, a long journey taken as an act of religious devotion.

The adventure began when we left Minneapolis on an overnight Icelandair flight to Reykjavik. Iceland itself is a legendary fishing destination for Atlantic salmon and large brown trout. After a few hours' layover we boarded another jet and flew to London's Heathrow. It was a beautiful day for flying. Nothing but smooth air and fair-weather cumulus clouds hung over the long blue miles of north Atlantic between Iceland and the United Kingdom. I dozed in the bright sunshine, six miles high.

Then Teresa was prodding me; we had crossed the English coast. I looked out of the window and was immediately struck by the mosaic of greens and yellows on the medieval fields and meadows laid out below us. The same distinctive patterns can be seen in gun-camera films taken by spitfires and mustangs during World War II. Thankfully there were no black-crossed Me-109s off our wingtips this day, but I scanned the sky anyway. I looked again at the green carpet unrolling beneath us. In my mind the words of William Blake and the music of C. Hubert Parry began to echo.

> And did those feet in ancient time,
> Walk upon England's mountains green.

This happened often during our trip. I'd be strolling along a footpath beside a river or walking up a cobbled village high street, and from somewhere words and music that I'd studied years before would form spontaneously in my mind, triggered by the surroundings.

Heathrow was a typical airport. The sleepy customs official's greatest concern seemed to be confirming that we did indeed have a hotel reservation for the evening, and soon we were on our way. Thankfully all of our checked baggage arrived safely, even the long rod case that housed our two-piece, nine-foot fly rods. I learned later that very few rods are actually stolen during air travel. More commonly the round rod tubes simply roll off the luggage conveyor belts and are lost in transit. Rod cases that are square or rectangular in cross-section don't roll easily and almost always reach their destination.

With our baggage in tow we boarded a bus that would take us from Heathrow to a train station in the suburb of Woking. Initially the bus ride was routine and unremarkable, but suddenly it was as if somebody had turned off a light switch. The sky was blotted out as the bus barreled along through a deep green tunnel. London was behind us and we were getting our first sight of English boundary hedges.

If good fences make good neighbors, the British may be the most neighborly folks in the world. Many hedges were fifteen to twenty feet high and sometimes, as in Woking, they stretched right over the highway from one side to the other. No one trims the interior square where the road goes through; the lorries (trucks) do that automatically and the effect is striking.

We left the bus in front of the railway station and trundled our luggage to the platform where we could catch a train southwest to Axminster in Dorset. Lots of signs warned us not to stand too close to the edge of the platform, and when the first express whistled through the station at eighty-five miles per hour we took the warning to heart. The draft from the passing train could have lifted a child or small adult right off their feet. We found that buses and trains in the UK ran exactly on schedule, speeding up or slowing down as needed so they would arrive at their destination *precisely* on time.

Jet lag began to catch up with me as our train rolled along, but I stayed awake and took in every detail of the landscape passing by. No student of fishing history could sleep through his or her first sight of the counties of Hampshire, Wiltshire, and Dorset. This is limestone country, a geology that raises the blood pressure of fossil hunters and trout fishers alike. The "matching the hatch" style of dry fly fishing was pioneered by fly fishers in the south and west of England during the late nineteenth and early twentieth centuries. Legendary anglers Frederic M. Halford and George Selwyn Marryat codified the theory and practice of dry fly fishing on the Rivers Test and Wylye near Winchester. Halford was the writer. Marryat was widely regarded as the most skillful fly fisher of his generation.

Meanwhile on the River Itchen, George Edward MacKenzie Skues worked out the principles of upstream nymph fishing for trout, principles that were fine tuned and expanded upon by Frank Sawyer, a keeper on the River Avon during the mid-twentieth century. Dorset was the home ground of a youthful Roderick L. Haig-Brown before he followed his destiny to Vancouver Island and the Pacific Northwest.

For me the high point of the train journey came when we crossed a small chalkstream that ran beneath a high viaduct between Basing-stoke and Andover. This was the little River Bourne that looms much larger in legend than it does in fact, having been immortalized by Harry Plunket Greene in his fly-fishing classic, *Where the Bright Waters Meet*. Spring creeks, no matter how small, are loved by trout anglers everywhere and in every time.

It was late afternoon when we left the train at Axminster and caught the bus down to Lyme Regis on the channel coast. Finally we rolled and hauled our luggage up a steep hill to the thatch-roofed Kersbrook Hotel, having traveled some four thousand miles in the past twenty-four hours. A European robin flashed from its perch in the garden as we entered and stacked our bags next to an enormous ammonite fossil that leaned against a bench. Teresa and I spent two days in Lyme Regis, slowly acclimating to a new place and a new culture that would be our home for the next month. Even in this relatively secluded corner of the United Kingdom there were wonders. The writer John Fowles lived just down the street from the Kersbrook and I thought about waiting nearby to see if I could talk to him or get his autograph. Writers must write about what they know, and Lyme Regis has several landmarks that feature in Fowles's best-known novel, *The French Lieutenant's Woman.*

We wandered down to the harbor and walked along the causeway known as the Cobb, which novelist Jane Austen describes in her classic *Persuasion.* Looking west along the shore in the clear morning we could see the Jurassic shale formation called the Undercliff, where Mary Anning and her family collected fossils during the early nineteenth century. Mary Anning discovered the first fossil ichthyosaurs and plesiosaurs at a time when women were mostly barred from doing science. Fossils were everywhere in Lyme Regis. We saw a complete ichthyosaur skeleton gathering dust in the display window of a little pharmacy on the village high street. Any museum in the world would have died to have that specimen. Many of Mary Anning's personal effects, including one of her rock hammers and pages from her journals, are preserved in the Lyme Regis Museum.

The rhythms and habits of life in the UK were interesting. We noted that Britons tended to pay for things in coin, maybe because they had coins in denominations up to two pounds sterling (about four American dollars at the time). Britons were strikingly thin, no doubt from all the walking they did. It was routine to see families with young children lugging huge picnic hampers on hikes up to four miles one way, just to have lunch outdoors on some picturesque knoll. Tort law seemed to be unknown; if you did something stupid and got hurt, or worse, it was your own damned fault. Signs on the moors (grassy uplands that do triple duty as national parks, grouse hunting areas, and aerial gunnery ranges) warned "Do not touch any military ordnance, as it may explode and kill you." Most of the English ways of doing things were sensible in the context of a small island shared by some sixty million people. We would find the same was true with regard to the fishing.

We were able to take a cab from Lyme Regis to Exeter Airport, where we rented a car and continued our journey southwest to the counties of Devon and Cornwall. Driving was an adventure that was much more difficult for the passenger than the driver. If something happened I could deal with it, but Teresa could only hold on tight and pray. Rural roads in Britain were generally much too narrow for the bus and truck traffic that used them. Somehow everybody got along, but not without some exciting moments. Hedges and stone walls came right up to the edge of the pavement; there was no shoulder. However, we were surprised to find that driving on the left was easy. Maybe too easy; when we got home, Teresa innocently began driving to Baraboo on the left side of the road. Shifting with the left hand was not so easy, and almost all rental cars in the UK had manual transmissions. Roundabouts at intersections were confusing at first. We had to be prepared to come to a full stop and yield to traffic coming from the right at every roundabout, including "mini-roundabouts," which were just circles and arrows painted on the roadway. Rural roads had signs, but the signs didn't tell us what road we were on. They told us which way to go to get to a particular village. If you try it, plan ahead and write a checklist of the villages you will pass through on your way from point A to point B. Above all, drive slowly and don't be discouraged. We found the freedom to go anywhere, in a foreign country, at our own pace was intoxicating.

It was late in the afternoon when we wheeled into the village of Lifton, in Devon. Lifton is what Grandmother would have called a "stone's throw town," meaning she could throw a stone from one end of it to the other. At the heart of Lifton is a massive gray building that has catered to travelers for hundreds of years, and to hunters and anglers for generations. Troops of jackdaws squeak a loud greeting to visitors as they arrive. A modest sign identifies the Arundel Arms, the quintessential British sporting hotel described so brilliantly by American author and editor Edward Weeks.

Ted Weeks edited the *Atlantic Monthly* (now the *Atlantic*) from 1938 to 1966, the longest tenure of any editor of the magazine. Weeks was a great discoverer of talented writers, like James Hilton, who wrote the modern classic *Good-bye, Mr. Chips*. Weeks authored several books, including *Fresh Waters*, a book of fishing stories that appeared in 1968. Like many people he discovered fishing relatively late in life and quickly fell under its spell. His stories included an extensive chapter on fishing in Britain, and when I read them for the first time a desire formed in my heart to stay at the Arundel Arms and fish the local spate rivers, such as the Lyd, Wolf, Tamar, and Ottery. Spate rivers are what we would call freestone streams, fed mostly by surface runoff.

In 2004, Anne Voss-Bark still owned and operated the Arundel Arms as she had since 1961, and she was one of my fly-fishing heroes. In her own book, *West Country Fly Fishing*, she collected and edited a series of fishing essays about the local region from an amazingly diverse set of authors. Among them were brilliant fishermen like Brian Clarke, Dermot Wilson, David Pilkington, and Conrad Voss-Bark; writers like the poet Ted Hughes; and salt-of-the-earth West Country men like Roy Buckingham, who recently retired from his position as fishing instructor and riverkeeper at the Arundel Arms after thirty-nine years of service. To our delight, right after we checked into the hotel, Anne Voss-Bark herself greeted us and joined us in the Arundel bar for drinks and a light snack. It was a conversation I will remember happily for the rest of my life.

Around us the bar was decorated with sporting memorabilia, including a display of photos, flies, and pages from the fishing journal of Major Oliver Kite, who popularized the now-famous Pheasant Tail Nymph. According to local legend, Major Kite made something of a nuisance of himself when he befriended Frank Sawyer, keeper of the Officer's Fishing Association water on the Hampshire Avon.

Sawyer happened to live across the street from Kite in the village of Netheravon, and even today there is talk among older folks in the pubs that much of the material in Kite's book, *Nymph Fishing in Practice,* was taken directly from Sawyer, a modest man of modest means. It was a bit of a thorn in Sawyer's side to look across the street and see the shiny white Jaguar XKE parked in front of the Kite residence, purchased with royalties from *Nymph Fishing in Practice* and also from the popular BBC television series *In Kite's Country.* Envy and politics play a part in every human endeavor, and fishing is no exception.

Anne Voss-Bark was everything a fly-fishing hero should be: amiable, gracious, fun loving, with a razor-sharp wit and a lovely smile. Winner of the "Woman Hotelier of the Year" and "Sporting Hotel of the Year" awards, she took considerable time from her busy schedule to talk to two Americans who were far from home, and she made us feel welcome at the end of a hard day when we really needed a friend. Teresa and I will always be grateful for that.

The next day was overcast with occasional rain showers. For the first time, we threw our fishing gear in the boot (trunk) of the car and went fishing in England. Our "beat," or assigned stretch of water, was the River Lyd, from its junction with the larger River Tamar upstream to the next bridge. We knew about the English beat system, which ensured that each angler fishing the hotel water had his or her own stretch of water to fish, but we were somewhat concerned about how much water that would turn out to be. These concerns vanished when we stepped over a stone wall via a wooden stile and got the first look at our beat.

The narrow valley of the River Lyd stretched out before us, lined with fields of barley across the uplands and forested in the lower elevations near the water. The junction with the Tamar was more than a mile away from where we stood, and it was at least a half-mile upstream to the road crossing. Our beat wasn't very limited. Hand-in-hand we walked across emerald green meadows and pastures bordered with flower-studded hedgerows toward the line of the Tamar. A herd of Holstein dairy cows chewed their cud and took no notice of us as we passed by. It all looked eerily like home. Sometimes we felt as if we could just drive back to Durwards Glen when we were done fishing, but the feeling passed when we reached the junction of the rivers. For a moment we stood poised on the ancient boundary between Devon and Cornwall, nearly all of it contested by dint of sword on shield in earlier days. Then we turned back into Devon and began wading and fishing the River Lyd.

The Lyd was entrenched between cliffs of dark, finely layered shale and slate. The banks were covered with ferns where the slope wasn't too steep, but in places ladders were provided so that anglers could reach the better pools. Thick belts of oak, beech, and ash covered both banks, and the limbs of the larger trees arched all the way across the river, leaving just a few patches where the sky was visible. The river was clear but tea stained with tannic acid from its peat bog beginnings on Dartmoor. We were struck by the sudden changes in the character of the water as we worked our way upstream. Great care had to be taken while wading, because the water could be ankle or shin deep in one place and suddenly drop off into a twelve-foot-deep hole on the very next step. It was hard to read the water.

Some likely looking places seemed not to have any fish at all, but then we would spook trout, both sea run and resident brown trout, from shallower areas where we didn't expect them to hold. In fact, we were learning a hard lesson that the farther one travels to fish, the more important it is to spend some time with a local guide in order to be successful. In previous fishing trips across North America we had done very well with Wisconsin flies and Wisconsin methods, but it was clearly a different ball game in the West Country of England.

Playing a hunch that attractor nymphs would provoke more strikes from trout in this relatively sterile stream, I fished a two-fly rig with a #14 Bead-head Pink Squirrel Nymph at the end of a 5x tippet with a #14 Partridge and Hare's Ear Soft Hackle on a dropper. A small strike indicator completed the rig, and I confidently waded to a good position downstream from the head of a good run. Sure enough, on only the second or third pitch into the run the indicator bobbed and I struck a very good fish. Roy Buckingham had told us that resident trout ran small in the local streams, and that anything eight inches or more was a good fish. My trout was easily a foot long, but as I brought it in it began to look strange and I soon realized that I hadn't caught a trout at all. When the fish was played out I lifted it from the water and there in my hand was a beautiful European grayling, almost a pound in weight, with red and blue highlights reflecting off its signature sail-like dorsal fin. In the back of my mind I'd hoped to catch a grayling somewhere in the UK, and here it was—my first fish of the trip and the first grayling of my life. For a Wisconsin angler, catching a grayling means you've traveled far and probably had many adventures, and so it proved for me.

When we reeled up in the evening and hiked back to the car, the grayling was the only decent fish that either of us had caught. A few tiny brown trout, or possibly Atlantic salmon parr, four to six inches long were the only other fish we had taken. Back at the Arundel Arms, another whole cadre of anglers was tackling up and setting off for the river. They were after *sea trout*, anadromous brown trout, which are mainly caught at night in this part of the UK. The best West Country rivers work hard. Fish in the Lyd and the Tamar can expect to see flies going past them every hour of the day and night during the prime part of the season.

I never did catch a large sea trout from the River Lyd, though I hooked several of them on a variety of flies during the daytime. The sea-run browns of the West Country are the only fish I've hooked in fresh water that could beat a Wisconsin smallmouth bass in a straight pound-for-pound fight. Violent is the word that best describes a fight with a sea trout. I lost sea trout in every possible way: they jumped and threw the fly, they jumped and landed on the fragile tippet, they rubbed the fly out on rocks, they cut the leader on rocks, and one heart-breaker ran upstream under a bridge and cut the leader on a piece of metal sticking out from the concrete.

The next day dawned clear and sunny, wretched weather for catching trout but wonderful for sightseeing, so Teresa and I drove across the moors to Land's End, the most southwesterly point of land in England. The rugged Cornwall coast is still one of the most sparsely populated areas in England. The continuous roar of towering waves crashing into the near-vertical headlands made it hard to talk to each other, and we sat atop the cliffs for a long time watching greater black-backed gulls ride the thermals and updrafts. The air was heavy with the salt smell of the sea, and only the cries of gulls and other sea birds rose and fell above the booming surf.

When we returned to the hotel, I walked across the garden to a hexagonal stone building with a rooster weathervane on the peak of the roof. The structure dated to the fourteenth century and was originally a cock-fighting pit, but was now a fully stocked fly shop. Roy Buckingham was more concerned about our relatively poor showing on the Lyd than we were, and he encouraged us to wet a line in Tinhay Lake that evening.

Tinhay Lake is a flooded limestone quarry at the bottom end of the village, and the trout we saw there were a marvel. In still-water trout fishing, England can justly claim to be world class. Cruising the margins of the blue-green lake were brown trout and rainbows in the five- to ten-pound class. Teresa and I are old hands with trout in lakes and ponds, and as we rigged our fly rods we chattered like little kids on Christmas Eve. This was going to be easy.

It wasn't. Yet again we showed British trout every fly in our boxes without generating a flicker of interest from the fish. Some kids fishing nearby caught a couple of rainbow trout by stripping Woolly Buggers on sinking lines, but their fish were only about fifteen inches long. I smiled when I thought how we treasure a fifteen-inch trout from the small spring creeks of Wisconsin, but the game changes immediately when larger fish are a possibility.

After a couple of hours our leaders had lengthened to nearly twenty feet and our flies had shrunk to various midges on size 22 to 28 hooks. I finally did manage to catch two rainbows, on a #24 Midge

Pupa tied to the end of a 7x tippet. The first trout was thirteen inches, but the second was twenty-two inches and when weighed in the net proved to be a few ounces over five pounds! It felt good to get that fish, and I was happy and contented as I walked along the lake to a grassy area at the lower end, near a vertical limestone cliff.

There was a place where the angler's path cut through a belt of brush and small trees that came right down to the water's edge. I scanned the shallows casually as I passed by. Suddenly I froze, and looked more intently. The glare of the low sun on the water was severe in that place, at that time of day, but with the benefit of polarized sunglasses I had caught just a glimpse of a long, silver shape with black spots moving slowly beneath the surface of the lake. A nonangler would never have seen it or would have dismissed this silver-on-silver flicker as a trick of the light and moved on. But I waited and watched intently. A few minutes later there was the same shape moving by very close to the bank, and then turning smoothly out and away to deeper water.

When it had gone I moved right to the water's edge and stood still again, watching with an intensity of purpose seen in herons, otters, kingfishers, and anglers. Sure enough, the trout swam by again in a few minutes and this time I could see that it was a brown trout about a yard long. Believe me or not if you wish, but I'd seen brown trout of similar proportions in Lake Michigan. This was a small lake in a typical English village.

It was pointless to fish for this trout with a 7x tippet, so I cut back and rebuilt the leader to 5x and tied on a classic British fly that was made for this situation; a #16 Pheasant Tail Nymph. It was impossible to make a conventional cast from this brushy place, and in any case the big brown was likely to swim right past my feet if I was patient. I extended the nine-foot rod as far out as I could reach and dapped the fly onto the water. Then I lowered the rod tip and watched it sink. The nymph was lost in the glare, but I kept watching the water where I thought it should be.

The fly couldn't have sunk more than a foot before a chunky one-pound rainbow hammered it, chewed it for a few seconds, and then spit it out. Then another rainbow of similar size charged in and did the same thing. Again I refrained from striking, and the trout eventually spit out the barbless Pheasant Tail and swam off in a huff. Minutes passed, minutes that felt like years. All at once I realized I was looking at a huge silverback with dime-sized spots, suspended motionless in the water about where my fly should be. I struck, and the surface of the lake erupted.

I can see it now as I write, frame by slow-motion frame: a cloud of spray like shining pearls, and a gigantic, hook-jawed trout suspended in the midst of it all. Its adipose fin flopped to and fro like a hunk of leather as large as a man's thumb. Then the great fish slapped back into the water and shot away on a reel-screeching run almost straight down into the depths. As the backing whistled through the guides I learned that Tinhay Lake was about ninety feet deep. I didn't really expect to land that trout. I just smiled wistfully when the 5x tippet finally popped beneath the weight and drag of thirty yards of weed-fouled fly line pulled through the water at speed. A yard-long salmon or trout from Lake Michigan weighs about fifteen pounds, and that's what I think this trout would have weighed, probably the largest inland brown trout I've ever tangled with in the course of a long and happy fishing life.

That evening I got an after-dinner drink from the bar and spent some time in the hotel's "common room." Classic tackle was displayed in glass cases here and there, and a battery of ancient fly rods made of greenheart and lancewood were mounted on the walls. One of the wooden rods even had a few yards of horse-hair fly line strung through the guides. No distinction was made regarding methods; spinning, casting, and fly tackle were displayed together, and there were pictures of all these sorts of tackle being used on local rivers and streams. How different from America, I thought, where people who fly fish often have little to say to those who use spinning rods and vice versa. In America we tend to ruin our rotator cuffs fly fishing at all costs in all places. UK anglers are more likely to select the tool to fit the job and adjust their fishing methods to suit the conditions. Yes, there are some British streams, typically chalkstreams in the south of England, which are restricted to upstream dry fly and nymph only. But when we fished those streams we found that the rules made sense *in those places.*

Always we came back to our amazement that the landscape around us in Devon and Cornwall looked so much like southwestern Wisconsin, even though the fishing was very different. We mentioned this to Roy Buckingham and he had a ready answer: Devon and Cornwall are the only counties in England that weren't covered by glaciers during the last ice age. We were fishing England's Driftless Area.

Days on the Dove

Do you think it will rain today?" Teresa asked our host during breakfast. I was too busy enjoying a tasty Dovedale sausage to join the conversation. "There now," said the innkeeper as he gestured expansively through the tall windows next to our table and across the grass-grown sheep pastures that surrounded the little white-washed hotel. "Do you see that green height off to the northeast? That's Thorpe Cloud that is. When you can see Thorpe Cloud it's going to rain, and when you can't see it, it's raining." We were at the Izaak Walton Hotel in the heart of the Derbyshire Peak. Two hundred feet below us the historic River Dove purled and growled along the limestone floor of the dale, in a chasm so deep that evening shadows fell at midday. How could I not fall in love with a river that has defied developers, road builders, and "progress" for centuries? Even today only a gravel footpath parallels the stream for much of its length.

The Dove is much more than a pristine trout river flowing through one of England's finest national parks. It looms larger in fly-fishing legend than any other trout stream on earth but one: ancient Macedonia's River Astraeus, whose true identity and location have been lost over the millennia since the Roman Claudius Aelianus set down the first written description of fly fishing for trout. The Astraeus has become a river of the imagination. The Dove is a river of reality. On the Dove you can lift a handful of icy water and let it run through your fingers back into the stream. You can smell it, listen to it, fish it, and become one with it.

The legend of the River Dove began in February 1676, when, "in a little more than ten days' time," Charles Cotton wrote the second part of Izaak Walton's classic, *The Compleat Angler*. Walton was a generalist who appreciated all forms of fishing with rod and line. There are chapters about fishing for grayling, salmon, trout, pike, perch, eels, and a wide variety of cyprinids, including tench, carp, chub, and barbel. But among some forty pages devoted to trout fishing, barely seven deal specifically with fly fishing, and Walton borrowed (some say plagiarized, but the practice was much more accepted in Walton's day) much of this material from earlier writers like Thomas Barker. Even in the seventeenth century there was more that could be said about *How to Angle for a Trout or Grayling in a Clear Stream*, and Walton knew that his good friend Charles Cotton was the man to say it.

What we know about Cotton's life illustrates the fine line that many people walk between a passion for fishing and an obsession. Thirty-seven years younger than Walton, Cotton has been described as "the dissolute aristocrat, the spendthrift courtier, [and] writer of obscene poetry." In most respects, except for politics and a true love of fishing, he was quite different from Walton. Yet somehow these two men became the best of friends. I like to think they met on the river, since no bonds of friendship are as strong as those forged between trout friends. Tangible evidence for this still stands beside the Dove a few miles above Dovedale. There, near the ruins of Beresford Hall, stands the red brick fishing house built by Charles Cotton in the late seventeenth century. The initials "IW" and "CC" are carved in cipher above the door.

Teresa and I knew that the present owner of the fishing house didn't allow visitors, so we contented ourselves with a few nights' stay at the Izaak Walton Hotel near Ashbourne. The hotel had limited fishing rights on the Dove downstream from Ilam Rock, and by booking early we were able to secure "a rod" on this historic water. The view from our upstairs room was magnificent and, surprisingly, a little eerie. I couldn't quite figure out why until I returned home and opened my reprint of the 1897 Le Gallienne edition of *The Compleat Angler*. There was an illustration of Dovedale "Below Thorpe Cloud," and it was precisely the same as the view from our window in 2004. That night our room was filled with the echoes of water cascading down the steep-walled valley. I could hardly sleep in the knowledge that tomorrow I would literally follow in the footsteps of two of the greatest anglers in history. When I finally did sleep, all of my dreams were haunted by sounds of falling water.

Naturally it was no trouble to be up and about at first light next morning. A gray, unfamiliar, dripping world cloaked in mist enveloped me as I walked from the hotel to the car park to tackle up. Never was

I happier to see my old trout rod, a handsome nine-foot graphite stick with a Peerless reel at the bottom. Familiar tackle is a comfort to a stranger in a strange land, and I never pick up that rod today without a few visions of England flitting through my mind.

Teresa joined me just as I finished rigging up with a #16 Pheasant Tail Nymph on a long 5x tippet, and we made our way down to the river. There was an interesting little path marked with white stones that headed straight across the fields from the hotel toward the Dove, but faced with the mist and the unfamiliar terrain we elected to follow the gravel road down from the car park. Several large parking areas border the Dove at the foot of Dovedale, and if the place is in any real danger from the twenty-first century it is the danger of being loved to death. On July weekends after school lets out for the summer holiday, Dovedale and the surrounding heights are absolutely packed with families picnicking, playing in the shallows with inflatable toys, hiking the footpath beside the river, throwing stones, catching snails, and swimming in the broader pools like the Nursery Pool upstream from the hotel. Quality fishing on summer weekends is out of the question. But in the gray dawn on this misty Monday morning the car parks were empty and we were alone with the river, perhaps the river of all rivers, wellspring of powerful water-magic that we call fishing. It felt as if we had discovered something ancient and valuable that had been lost for a long time. As we crossed the Dove on the stepping stones we were very conscious of leaving the workaday world behind us and entering that dimension only anglers know.

My first impression of the Dove was that it was a cross between a valley spring creek and a mountain freestone trout stream. Steep, rocky heights studded with gnarled fir trees soared above us and lost themselves in mist. Below them the river chattered noisily as it snaked across its stony bed. But the stones were limestone and dolomite, and in several places large springs emerged from caves and fissures to add their strength to the gathering flood. It was a hot summer in England that year, but water temperatures in the Dove stayed around fifty-five degrees Fahrenheit all through the long, sunny afternoons as trout twisted scuds off of rocks on the bottom.

The water itself was clear in the shallows and at the tails of pools, but dissolved minerals produced a deep translucent blue in the deeper holes. Twenty to forty feet wide, the Dove was too deep to wade in some places, while in others the banks were too steep to walk on. This made it a challenge to fish, so we contented ourselves with fishing wherever the well-worn anglers' paths took us. No doubt they took us to pools and runs that Walton and Cotton knew well. As our lines rolled out across the azure Dove, those heady days of the Restoration no longer seemed so far off.

Our tackle differed markedly from the gear that Walton and Cotton carried to the stream. No reels graced their pliant rods, rods that were double the length of ours and constructed from a carefully selected variety of woods. Lines of plaited horsehair tapered down to just a single hair tied to the fly, which Cotton often made by hand while standing on the riverbank. This wasn't as hard as it seems. Cotton's flies were laughably simple creations compared with flies shown in today's tackle catalogs. Many were just a dubbed fur body with a pair of wings. Despite this simplicity, Cotton attempted to imitate specific aquatic and terrestrial insects, including mayflies, "cadis" (caddis), ants, and grasshoppers. Other flies were attractors chosen according to weather and water conditions. Cotton's "palmer flies" were direct ancestors of the popular Woolly Buggers of our own time.

It's a mistake to think that accomplished anglers of the past were less intelligent or sophisticated than those of today. In many ways they were more skilled and resourceful, more self-reliant and confident of their abilities than we are. At a time when tackle shops were few and synthetic materials unknown, people crafted their own fishing gear with their own hands from whatever materials nature provided. Remember the satisfaction of that first good trout caught with a fly of your own making? Or perhaps the feeling of walking up to your first whitetail buck taken with the whistling flight of an arrow fletched by your own hands, from a bow constructed patiently over many a dark winter night? Folk were fewer in Cotton's day, but more of them knew and loved these things.

With their willowy rods and horsehair lines, seventeenth-century anglers were largely at the mercy of the wind. Whether they fished upstream or down depended on the set of the wind on a given day irrespective of other tactical considerations. Upstream or down, Cotton was well aware of the need to keep trout and grayling from detecting the angler's presence. "To fish fine and far off is the first and principal rule for trout angling," so Teresa and I moved slowly along the banks of the Dove, watching every piece of likely water for several minutes before making the first cast.

Sometimes we could see trout holding near the surface of the river. Their tails and fins rippled in anticipation of some choice insect coming down to them, either afloat or awash in a bubble line. Dry flies were the obvious choice for these fish. More often we drifted weighted nymphs through the deeper places and struck many a good trout unseen from above.

Large spires and pinnacles of limestone towered over many of the better pools; at eighty-two feet, Ilam Rock was the tallest of these. Again I heard Cotton's voice as I waded the river and cast my flies: "These hills, though high, bleak, and craggy, breed and feed good beef and mutton above ground and afford good store of lead within." How like our home in southwestern Wisconsin, I thought, right down to the veins of lead permeating the bedrock.

Walton and Cotton seemed closer too. For hundreds of years people have enjoyed wandering the countryside in pursuit of trout, sometimes in their home waters, sometimes farther off. If it were simply a matter of catching trout to eat, very little would be written about fishing. But as Roderick L. Haig-Brown once wrote, "The fishing is far more important than the fish." There is the fun of anticipation as tackle is prepared. Maps are studied with the intensity of a military campaign, and detailed plans are discussed at length. The experience of traveling to the waterside at dawn, fishing through much of the day, and finally returning home again in the evening immerses the angler in nature and fosters a spirit of contemplation. Sometimes one goes through an entire day without seeing or speaking to another human being. There is satisfaction in the exercise of skill, in casting and fishing well even if no fish are caught. But the excitement of hooking a good fish and fighting it to the net with a rod is an excitement that never fades, no matter how many years have passed since one's first trout was taken. I still quiver like an aspen leaf in a September breeze when I strike a good trout on the fly, just as I did when I was a boy (indeed, perhaps more). The reward is the living jewel of a trout in the hand, the sheen of the river written in its silver scales, golden gravel reflected in its yellow flanks, red dots glowing like fiery coals on its sides. There are things on this good earth that only the angler sees, and one of them is the breathless beauty of a trout emerging from a river. Time passes, but some things endure.

Auld Red

There once was a wise, fat, red-golden brown trout that lived for many years in the River Test where it runs through the village of Whitchurch, in Hampshire. The trout's name was Auld Red and he was the most famous fish in the village. I like to think he lives there still. Auld Red was clearly a Trout of the Cloth, because his favorite haunt was a deep cut just across the lawn from the parish church. Here the wayward Test had undercut the church-yard wall until a part of it collapsed into the river, and the vicar, a man who understood that rivers are the veins of God, was content to leave well enough alone. Besides, everybody in the village, including the vicar and the riverkeeper, liked to sit on the stone bench beside the well-worn footpath and watch the trout and grayling that fed in the deep cut along the ruined wall. And among the many fish that jockeyed for choice positions in the cut, Auld Red reigned like a king among peasants.

Whitchurch is one of those delightful little villages that can still be found in the south of England, *if* one has the courage to drive out of Greater London and explore the countryside. Daily life in Whitchurch hasn't changed much in a thousand years. In February the gates on the Test are opened and the water-meadows submerge in a knee-deep flood of tea-colored water. Once the new grass is green and growing, the gates are closed, the Test clears, the trout retire to the carriers, and the sheep are turned out to feast. Then comes the mayfly interlude, sometimes called the "duffer's fortnight," when large trout lose some of their native caution and chase the dancing armada of mayflies with reckless abandon. Finally summer comes in, and life in the Test valley takes on a serene, lazy quality; all is green and warm and comfortable.

It was high summer when I came down to Whitchurch with Duncan Weston. Duncan is a white-haired giant of a Scot who's also a giant among fishing companions. He guides on the chalkstreams by choice, having retired from a notably successful career at IBM some fifteen years ago. We hit it off immediately on the first day we fished together, and by the end of the second day we were a team. Each of us carried a fly rod; one was rigged with a dry fly (usually a #18 Parachute Adams), the other with a nymph (most often a #16 Sawyer Pheasant Tail). Each of us searched the water diligently for hints and indications of trout, since the rules on most of the Test allow casting only to trout that can be seen. And with patient observation, most of the trout told us not only where they were but also how to catch them. Fish grubbing the bottom might vacuum a deep-drifting nymph, while trout looking up with fins aquiver were ideal candidates for the aristocratic dry fly.

Duncan warned me on the drive over from Stockbridge that the fishing wouldn't be easy. "The rod average at Whitchurch is less than four fish per day, trout and grayling taken together," he said. "But we'll speak to the riverkeeper and have a go!" Chas, the keeper, met us at the Fulling Mill where he and his family lived in the ground-floor rooms. In the United Kingdom, a riverkeeper is both gardener and guardian of his trout stream. Most live right beside the river they work, and a good part of every keeper's day is spent outdoors in all seasons.

On the chalkstreams, riverkeepers selectively cut weeds (to promote fly life and keep silt from building up), check anglers for permits and licenses, survey and manage trout stocks, remove pike, discourage poachers, and do what they can to promote bird and animal life in the valley. Such men develop a bond with the earth that may be unique in our twenty-first-century culture. A keeper knows a river's most intimate secrets, including where the big fish are.

It was a picture-perfect summer's day. I'd come to this reach of the Test in search of many things, trout and grayling among them. My day at Whitchurch was the fulfillment of a life-long dream: to visit the Fulling Mill where Harry Plunket Greene, a famous public singer and author of the fly-fishing classic *Where the Bright Waters Meet*, once rented a flat, and to throw a fly over the renowned River Test in the same reach that Plunket Greene himself had fished nearly a century before.

The July sun was high and bright, but the day was cool, and there was just enough breeze to push land-bred insects onto the water. I have been fortunate to fish many hallowed and famous trout rivers in my time, but I do not hesitate to say that the River Test on that day was the most wonderful river I have ever seen, and probably ever will see.

I stood in the shade of a tall beech tree, on the bank of a crystal-clear chalkstream some sixty feet wide. A grove of ancient beeches towered over the wide turn of the river above the Fulling Mill, their massive limbs reaching clear across from bank to bank. Rich beds of cress, starwort, and water crowfoot waved languidly in the current and split the Test into braided channels teeming with shrimp, mayfly, and caddis larvae. Each channel was floored with golden gravel that glittered and flashed in the dappled light, and in each channel were wild trout and grayling, some big and some small, some rising, some shrimping on the bottom, and others seemingly lulled to sleep by whispering leaves in the summer sunshine. And there we were, Duncan and I, with a whole day before us and nothing to do but fish.

I waded out into the smooth flow of the Test and searched the nearest channel for a target. A shoal of small grayling hovered nervously in the shallow tail-out, but there didn't seem to be anything above. Then, out of the corner of my eye I caught a wavy shimmer hard down among the stones. I waited, and I watched intently. And again there was movement, but this time, by a trick of the light and shadow and a lens of still water, I saw the broad back of a trout as it slithered out from under a weed mat, glided across the bottom of the channel, and vanished again beneath the weeds on the other side. I unhooked the little Pheasant Tail, worked out line, and cast the fly well upstream to the top of the run. The nymph sank quickly out of sight in the thigh-deep channel. I couldn't see the fly at all, but I watched the gravel bottom expectantly. Sure enough, just when I judged that the nymph should be bumping past its holt, the trout slithered out from beneath the weeds and sailed across the gravelly channel once more. I tightened, the rod bent, and a fat two-pound brown trout rose up from the bottom, gills flared, white mouth open wide, shaking its head in a spasm of anger and panic. What followed was a game of chess played out between the weed beds. When hooked, chalkstream trout often dive into the thickest, nastiest weeds they can find. If the fish is badly weeded, it is often possible to wade directly below the fish, pull on the leader by hand and extract the trout along the natural set of the vegetation. Judging by the way it power-dived from one weed bed to the next, this particular trout had won many battles. But not this one. Each time the fish weeded I was able to patiently hand-line him back out into relatively open water, and in the end I got him.

Fishing, like shooting, golf, and many other athletic pursuits, can be streaky. Some days we can't buy a fish, while on other days we can't seem to keep them from jumping into our nets. Thankfully my day at Whitchurch was one of the latter, and by lunchtime I'd already caught the "rod average" several times over. When we returned to the river after lunch, Duncan sent me upstream on my own for the better part of an hour while he and Chas visited back at the Mill. As Duncan told me later, Chas asked the usual questions about how the fishing was, whether we had seen trout or grayling in this place or that, and finally how I was doing with the notoriously fussy wild fish on the Fulling Mill beat of the Test. "That Yank's a bloody genius," Duncan replied. "A buggerin' bloody genius! Especially with a nymph." Chas sneered at that. Riverkeepers watch more people fish in a month than most fishermen do in a decade and they've heard every fish story a thousand times over, so I couldn't blame Chas for taking a jaded view. Besides, nearly all of all of my success was due to a string of lucky breaks coupled with Duncan's exceptional ability as a guide. "Well," said Chas with a rise of his bushy eyebrows, "if 'e's a *buggerin'* bloody genius, take 'im up to the cut boy the churchyard woll an' see if 'e can have Auld Red out. That bloody trout ain't so much as looked at a fly in a month o' Sundays!"

I was in the act of kissing a beautiful three-pound grayling (by far the largest I'd ever caught) when Duncan reappeared on the riverbank, his Scot's eyes shining and a positively wicked grin on his grizzled face. "You've been given a challenge, son!" he said. "Put yon carp back in the river; we're goin' up to the churchyard woll!" I waded over, and with one arm Duncan pulled me out of the water and right to the very top of the bank. Then he explained the situation as we walked upstream on the well-worn footpath beside the Test.

I abhor competition in my fishing, always and everywhere. And yet . . . I hadn't sought this challenge. It was also clear that Duncan viewed the situation as a personal challenge to himself, as guide, and woe unto him who challenges a Scot in a matter of honor, be he riverkeeper or no. I accepted the challenge.

We reached the stone bench beside the footpath and scanned the cut along the fallen churchyard wall. Just where a clump of willow stems leaned out over the river, in the very best lie at the very top of the cut, was Auld Red. His attitude seemed to be one of portly beneficence as he wallowed there in the slow eddy near the wall.

Frankly, Auld Red was morbidly obese. He seemed ancient; the bottom of his tail was worn away from years of sculling against the gravel, and he had a hooked kype at the tip of his lower jaw that completely missed the V-notch at the tip of his upper jaw and gave him a cheesy, out-of-balance grin that, on a trout, looked silly. But he was feeding; a sparse hatch of iron blue duns had broken out and Auld Red was putting on a clinic for "How to Be a Selective Trout." He'd let each dun drift around the eddy at the tip of his nose, and if the fly made a complete circle without lifting off and flying away, Auld Red would tip his fins imperceptibly and somehow take the dun with his bent-scissors jaws. We saw that Auld Red was locked on to "cripples," which was fortunate. As Duncan said while looking over my box of oh-so-carefully tied dries: "Bollocks, Kev—all yer flies are cripples!"

With my best "cripple" affixed to a long 6x leader I waded out to tilt with Auld Red for bragging rights on the Test. Eddies are tricky; experienced trout know very well that drag protects them, and they have a maddening habit of balancing the fly on their nose (without taking it), and then turning away with an "I-told-you-so" look once the fly drags and their suspicions are confirmed. Auld Red was no exception. I did my best imitation of a pile cast (so easy to do when I don't want to; so difficult to pull off when I do), and hoped for the best. I can still see it in my mind's eye: the leader landing in a heap on the water, then the "feathered Judas" floating down the eddy, flush in the surface film, then Auld Red coming to the fly, smiling that goofy, odd-ball smile . . . smiling . . . smiling . . . the fly reaching its limit of drift . . . drag just about to set in . . . and then Auld Red sucking in the fly, completely duped. The spotted son-of-a-gun won by flabbergasting me. Fully expecting a refusal, I came completely unhinged when Auld Red took the fly on the very first cast. Duncan leaped to his feet and let out a highland yell. I struck hard enough to cross the eyes of a billfish, but unfortunately I was fishing 6x nylon on the clear waters of the River Test and not a wire cable in the blue Pacific. I didn't even feel the tippet pop.

I'd have crawled under a rock, but rocks are few and far between on the Hampshire chalkstreams. Duncan commiserated with me as we sat on the stone bench, and I replaced the tippet and put on another fly, a Pheasant Tail Nymph this time. Auld Red was still in his lie at the top of the cut, but now the great trout rested on the bottom, frightened and a bit sullen, perhaps. For some reason Duncan and I stayed where we were on the stone bench, watching the river, not saying much. I honestly don't know how much time went by—a half-hour, an hour, or a lifetime. The bell in the parish church tolled five o'clock. And then Auld Red lifted himself off the bottom and shook himself back together. Where before his fins had been closed up tight against his body, now they were extended and quivering in the slow currents of the Test. Duncan said, "He might take a nymph. Try him again." I tried a half-dozen casts, but the little Pheasant Tail seemed to have lost its magic and Auld Red showed no interest. Maybe he'd seen too many Pheasant Tail Nymphs in his little corner of the world.

Duncan clipped the fly from the tippet and handed me a well-chewed mess of a fly from his own box. "It's a little Greenwell nymph. Seems to work well at this time of year." he said. I tied it on and waded into position once again, but without much conviction. How many times must a scenario be repeated before we react to it by reflex, unconsciously? I don't know: thousands, maybe tens of thousands of times. All I know is that Auld Red gave no indication that he'd taken the nymph, but suddenly my right arm came up and he was well and truly hooked. He may have resembled a pudgy village alderman, but Auld Red still had something of the tiger in him and the fight was not without moments of high drama. Time after time he surged upstream on blistering runs and then dogged deep, trying to saw the tippet or rub out the fly on pieces of sunken masonry.

I confess I let out a rebel yell when Auld Red was in the net at last. Duncan wore a smile so big I thought he might split at the ears. We didn't have a camera, but we certainly savored the moment as we stood there, in the middle of the River Test, while the Pride of Whitchurch recovered his equilibrium and his goofy grin. There was no question about releasing Auld Red; every village should have a trout with a name. A pair of big grayling, sensing opportunity, had hastily moved in and taken over his lie when Auld Red was pulled out, but they fell back downstream immediately when the boss of the hole came home.

At the end of the day I think Duncan wanted to run all the way back to the Mill. There was no need. Unable to wait for news, Chas had walked out to meet us on the footpath at dusk, and he immediately perceived what had happened even before we said anything. "You lucky *bastards!*" he said, but I could see him smiling in the last light of evening.